D1432438

The Psychology of Affiliation

STANFORD STUDIES IN PSYCHOLOGY, I

EDITORS
Robert R. Sears
Leon Festinger
Douglas H. Lawrence

STANLEY SCHACHTER

The Psychology of Affiliation

Experimental Studies of the Sources of Gregariousness

STANFORD UNIVERSITY PRESS • STANFORD, CALIFORNIA

NCMC
HM
251
.S298

Stanford University Press
Stanford, California
© *1959 by the Board of Trustees of the*
Leland Stanford Junior University
Printed in the United States of America
First published 1959
Last figure below indicates year of this printing:
77 76 75 74 73 72 71 70 69 68

Acknowledgments

The studies reported in this book were conducted at the Laboratory for Research in Social Relations of the University of Minnesota under grants from the Office of Naval Research and the National Institute of Mental Health. To both organizations, my gratitude for their generous support.

My assistants during most of these investigations were Roland Radloff and James Banks. To them both go my warmest thanks for their active collaboration in all phases of this research program. During the time these studies were being planned and carried out, Ben Willerman and Ragnar Rommetveit generously contributed their ideas and time to discussions of experimental design and interpretation. Morton Deutsch, Leon Festinger, Harold Kelley, and Robert Sears have read major sections of early forms of this manuscript and their suggestions have strongly influenced this final version. Finally, I wish to thank Ann Haeberle, Donald Stieper, and Paul Torrance all of whom have generously performed the special analyses of their own data required to test the points at issue in Chapter 6 of this volume.

Contents

The Psychology of Affiliation

1

*A*ffiliation and Isolation

Walt Whitman once wrote, "I . . . demand the most copious and close companionship of men." The sentiment is familiar, for most of us have experienced occasional cravings to be with people, sometimes for good reason, frequently for no apparent reason: we seem simply to want to be in the physical presence of others. Whatever the reasons, these desires that draw men together furnish the substance of the social sciences, which in good part are devoted to the study of the process and products of human association.

Despite the importance of the study of the affiliative needs, almost nothing is known of the variables and conditions affecting these needs. We have no precise idea of the circumstances that drive men either to seek one another out or to crave privacy, and we have only the vaguest and most obvious sort of suggestions concerning the kinds of satisfaction that men seek in company. A review of the literature indicates that there has been some psychoanalytic thought on the topic (39); that, at most, there have been two or three immediately relevant experiments; and, most prominently, that there has been a generous amount of common sense, mildly obvious formulation of the fact that people do associate (9, 19).

The gist of what we have called the "common sense" line of thought may be summarized in two propositions:

First, people do mediate goals for one another, and it may be necessary to associate with other people or belong to particular groups in order to obtain specifiable individual goals. For example, to hold a job it may be necessary to join a union; to play bridge it may be necessary to become a member of a bridge club;

and so on. Not surprisingly, a number of studies have demonstrated that the attractiveness of the group or of specific individuals will vary with their promised or proven success in facilitating goal attainment (26, 48). Certainly, a large if not major portion of our associational activities can be subsumed in this general class of affiliative behavior. It is a peculiarly asocial sort of affiliation that is under consideration, however, for people qua people may be considered as irrelevant. In these terms, a nonsocial means of goal attainment may be just as satisfactory and attractive as a social means. More cogent to present concerns is the substance of the following proposition.

Second, people, in and of themselves, represent goals for one another; that is, people do have needs which can be satisfied *only* in interpersonal relations. Approval, support, friendship, prestige, and the like have been offered as examples of such needs. There is no doubt that such needs are particularly powerful ones and that association with other people is a necessity for most of us.

The distinction drawn in these two propositions is hardly a sharp one, and one could quibble endlessly as to whether this is a distinction at all. The relative emphasis of the two propositions, however, is clear enough. In the one case, association represents a means to an essentially asocial goal; in the other, the gratifications, whatever they may be, of association itself represent the goal. It is our intention in this volume to concentrate on the latter type of associational activity and to attempt to spell out some of the circumstances and variables affecting the affiliative tendencies.

SOCIAL NEEDS

Perhaps the single study directly concerned with the experimental examination of specific needs which can be satisfied only by means of interpersonal contact is the study of Festinger, Pepitone, and Newcomb (17), where it is suggested that there are two classes of needs which group membership satisfies—needs such as approval, status, and help, which require singling the individual out and necessarily involve high social visibility and individual identifiability; and needs whose satisfaction requires being "submerged in the group," a condition labeled "de-individuation" and described as a state of personal anonymity in which the individual does not feel singled out or identifiable.

It is suggested that there are many kinds of behavior in which the individual would like to engage where activity is prevented by the existence of inner restraints. Instances of such behavior might be acting wildly and boisterously, "talking dirty," expressing hostilities, and so on. Festinger et al. suggest that under conditions where the individual is not "individuated" in the group, such restraints will be reduced and individuals will be able to satisfy needs which might otherwise remain unsatisfied. In an ingenious experiment, these authors demonstrate that the state of de-individuation in the group does occur and is accompanied by reduction of the inner restraints of the members of the group. Further, they demonstrate that groups in which such restraints are reduced are more attractive to their members than groups in which restraints are not reduced.

An entirely different set of needs that may be satisfiable only by association with other people is discussed by Festinger (15) in his theoretical paper on social comparison processes. Festinger writes:

> The drive for self evaluation concerning one's opinions and abilities has implications not only for the behavior of persons in groups but also for the processes of formation of groups and changing membership of groups. To the extent that self evaluation can only be accomplished by means of comparison with other persons, the drive for self evaluation is a force acting on persons to belong to groups, to associate with others. And the subjective feelings of correctness in one's opinions and the subjective evaluation of adequacy of one's performance on important abilities are some of the satisfactions that persons attain in the course of these associations with other people. How strong the drives and satisfactions stemming from these sources are compared to the other needs which people satisfy in groups is impossible to say, but it seems clear that the drive for self evaluation is an important factor contributing to making the human being "gregarious." (Pp. 135–136.)

This notion of a "drive for self evaluation" has slowly emerged as the theoretical underpinning for a schema and body of research on social influence. Essentially it has been assumed that, given such a drive, tendencies exist to establish the "rightness" or "wrongness" of an opinion and the "goodness" or "badness" of an ability. If it is possible to check against physical reality or against authoritative sources, such evaluation may be forthright and simple. More often than not, however, such evaluative resources are nonexistent and it is possible to evaluate only by reference to other people. One's ability is good or bad only in comparison with the ability of others; one's opinion may be evaluable as right or wrong only in terms of agreement or disagreement with the opinions held by other people. Such social evaluation is possible, however, only when the comparison points are relatively close to one's own position. A sandlot baseball player learns little about his ability as a batter by comparing himself with Willie Mays; he learns a great deal by comparing himself with his teammates. A Jew does not evaluate the correctness of his opinions of Zionism by comparing them with those of an Arab nationalist. It has been demonstrated (12, 16, 30) that stable evaluation of opinions or abilities is possible chiefly when those with whom comparison is made are quite close to one's own position. The greater the extent to which other people agree with one's opinion, the greater the feeling of correctness and the greater the stability of the opinion. This series of assumptions concerning the evaluation process leads to the expectation that when discrepancies of opinion or ability exist among the members of a group, tendencies will arise to reduce this discrepancy. Spelling out and testing the implications of this expectation, a series of experiments have been conducted in order to examine the conditions under which influence will be exerted by the group (3, 28, 36), influence will be accepted by the individual (3, 20), and deviates rejected by the group (36).

Though the assumption of a drive for evaluation of the opinions and abilities has proven particularly fruitful in generating research tests of its implications, whether or not such a drive is indeed a major source of "gregariousness" is still an open question, for there are, unfortunately, almost no studies bearing directly on the question. The single piece of research that is relevant is the case study by Festinger, Riecken, and Schachter (18) of a millenial group. This group had predicted, for a specific date, the destruction of the world as we know it through a series of earth-shaking cataclysms—a prediction which was not confirmed. The effect of this disconfirmation was, of course, to shake all confidence in the belief system which had led to this prediction. The almost immediate reaction to disconfirmation was a frenzy of attempts to convert and proselyte. Prior to disconfirmation, this group had been secretive and inhospitable, avoiding all publicity and contact with outsiders. Following disconfirmation, they exposed themselves to the world, called in newspapers, and worked furiously to convince possible converts—all, presumably, in an attempt to establish a new and firm social basis for their beliefs.

If one broadens this "drive for evaluation of opinions and abilities" into a more general "drive for cognitive clarity," one does find additional evidence for the proposition that evaluative or cognitive needs are an important source of affiliative behavior. There are many thoroughly ambiguous issues that are impossible to clarify by reference either to the physical world or to authoritative sources. For such issues, if one assumes a need for cognitive clarity, it is plausible to assume that attempts to reduce ambiguity will take the direction of intensive social contact and discussion. Evidence that this is indeed the case can be found as a by-product of a study of rumor transmission conducted by Schachter and Burdick (37). This study took place in a girls' school. In a deliberate attempt to create an event that would be mystifying and not readily explainable, the principal of the school went into several classrooms during first-hour classes, pointed at a single girl, and said, "Miss K., get your hat, coat, and books and come with me. You will be gone for the rest of the day." Nothing of this sort had ever occurred before and absolutely no explanation was offered. Not surprisingly, the remaining girls spent almost all of the school day in intensive social contact and communication in an attempt to clear up and understand what had happened.

Such is the research literature that has most immediately stimulated our interest in the topic—a handful of studies suggesting that people will seek one another out when their opinions are shaken; that an otherwise uninterpretable event leads to a search for social reality; and that association may lead to a state of relative anonymity allowing the satisfaction of needs which might otherwise remain unsatisfied. These are intriguing leads, but it is clear that our knowledge of conditions affecting affiliative behavior is still rudimentary.

Many other studies, of course, are tangentially related to present concerns. Atkinson (2) and French (22, 23) and their colleagues have devised measures of a generalized need for affiliation. Their experimental work, however, has been concerned chiefly with a comparison of specific behaviors of those high and low in affiliative needs. They have not as yet published research on the conditions and variables affecting the magnitude of the affiliative need. In addition to studies dealing explicitly with aspects of affiliation, studies of interpersonal communication and rumor spread, studies of panic, and studies of sociometric choice, community studies and analyses of organization behavior almost all rest on implicit assumptions as to the sources of affiliative behavior. However, most of these studies are concerned primarily with the consequences of association rather than with the reasons for association, and we shall not attempt to review studies peripherally related to our central concern.

SOCIAL ISOLATION

If such evidence is needed, an examination of the consequences of social isolation shows convincingly that the social needs are indeed powerful ones. Autobiographical reports of such people as religious hermits, prisoners of war, and castaways make it clear that the effects of isolation can be devastating. For example, a prisoner (52) writes, "Gradually the loneliness closed in. Later on I was to experience situations which amounted almost to physical torture, but even that seemed preferable to absolute isolation." (P. 89.) Such reports are extremely common and seem to be as typical of those who have gone into voluntary isolation as of those forced into solitary confinement. A religious solitary (1) describes the experience in these words:

> When the great resolution has been taken, to leave all and go in search of God in solitude, there comes that first-hour zest which attends all new undertakings begun with good will. That lasts as long as it ought to last; more shortly for big souls, longer for the lesser—it is the jam to get the powder down. Then begins the first revelation, and a very unpleasant one it is. The solitary begins to see himself as he really is. The meanness, the crookedness of natural character begins to stand out in a strong light; those wounds that disobedience to conscience in the past has left festering, now give forth their poisoned matter. There may be terrible uprisings of lower nature, and more formidable yet, resistance of self-will to the strait-jacket into which he would thrust it. Here you get the reason for what look like eccentricities of asceticism, its bread-and-water fasts, scourges and the rest, even to midnight immersions practiced by Celtic solitaries. It is Master Soul, the rider, whipping Brother Ass, the body, into obedience. This stage may last months or years; how long, no one can foretell; but while it lasts, solitude is full of strife and pain. (Pp. xv–xvi.)

Aside from these reports of profound disturbance, anxiety, and pain, the condition of absolute social deprivation as described in these autobiographical reminiscences seems responsible for many other dramatic effects. Most prominently, the following three trends characterize many of these reports:

First, the reported "pain" of the isolation experience seems typically to bear a nonmonotonic relationship to time—increasing to a maximum and then, in many cases, decreasing sharply. This decrease in pain is frequently marked by onset of a state of apathy sometimes so severe as to resemble a schizophrenic-like state of withdrawal and detachment, so marked in some cases that prisoners have to be physically removed from their cells (14). Indeed, this condition is so common that the Church recognizes the state of acedia (or sloth, one of the seven deadly sins) as an occupational disease of hermits. Draguet (11) in his volume on the desert fathers describes a mild form of this state as follows:

> L'acédie . . . est, en somme, l'état de dépression dans lequel l'ascète, pour quelque cause ou complexe de causes, physiques ou mentales . . . éprouve du vague à l'âme, de la lassitude, de la tristesse, de l'ennui, du découragement, voire du dégoût pour la vie spirituelle, qui lui apparaît monotone et sans but, pénible et inutile; l'idéal ascétique, soudainement obscurci, est sans force d'attraction; l'euphorie a disparu avec l'activité des puissances de l'âme. Si, au lieu d'opérer le redressement nécessaire, l'ascète ne réagit pas, il se met à négliger ses exercices: la *"ferveur"* fait place à la *"tièdeur."* (P. xxxvi.)

Second, there seems to be a strong tendency for those in isolation to think, dream, and occasionally hallucinate about people. Indeed, comparison of the anchoritic or hermit saints with the cenobitic saints indicates greater frequency of visions and hallucinatory experiences for the religious solitaries.

And third, those isolates who are able to keep themselves occupied with distracting activities appear to suffer less and be less prone to the state of apathy. Those prisoners who are able to invent occupations for themselves and schedule for themselves activities such as doing mental arithmetic or recalling poetry seem to bear up better under the experience than those who either think chiefly of their plight or dwell on the outside world. Needless to say, cause and effect are completely confounded in this relationship as stated, but Schönbach (40) in an experimental study addressed directly to this point has demonstrated that a state of deprivation is far more bearable under manipulated conditions of irrelevant and distracting thought than under conditions where thought is concerned almost wholly with the source of deprivation.

Though all of this is of absorbing interest, its interpretation is thoroughly confounded by the multitude of coacting variables and the indistinguishability of cause and effect; proper investigation of these various phenomena demands direct and controlled study. Several years ago, therefore, in a preliminary attempt to examine some of the consequences of social isolation, the author conducted a small series of isolation case studies. Student volunteers, who were paid ten dollars a day, were supplied with food and locked into a windowless room for periods ranging from two to eight days. Their watches and wallets were removed and their pockets emptied. Some subjects were provided with a variety of minor distracting devices, such as metal-link puzzles, dart boards, and so on. Other subjects were left completely to their own devices and entered a room barren of anything but a bed, a chair, a lamp, a table, and, unknown to the subject, a one-way observation mirror. In no case was a subject permitted books, radio, or any device that could directly serve as a social surrogate. For the period of isolation, all subjects were left completely to their own resources to spend their time as they would and with absolutely no communication with the experimenter or the outside world. In addition to these voluntary isolates, interviews were conducted with a few prisoners who, as punishment, were in solitary confinement cells at the Minnesota State Prison.

After the extremes of the autobiographical reports, this first-hand contact was sobering. The prisoners, who had been in solitary confinement for periods ranging from three to five days, were not particularly troubled by the experience; they were interested chiefly in bumming cigarettes and complaining about the food. As for the students, five subjects were run in the experimental isolation room. One subject broke down after two hours, almost hammering down the door to get out. Of three subjects who remained in isolation for a two-day period, one admitted that he had become quite uneasy and was unwilling to go through the experience again, while the other two subjects seemed quite unaffected by two days of isolation. The fifth subject was isolated for eight days. He admitted that by the end of this eight-day period he was growing uneasy and nervous, and he was certainly delighted to be able to see people again; but one could hardly describe his condition as having grown intolerable.

The results of these few case studies are clearly incompatible with the common report, in the autobiographies analyzed, that isolation is, at some point, an agonizingly painful process. Two explanations come readily to mind: the period of isolation is far longer for real-life isolates than for our subjects; and other variables, most of all fear, account for the extreme suffering of real-life isolates.

Neither of these explanations seems to suffice. Though fear is certainly a reasonable alternative explanation for such isolates as prisoners of war, it can hardly be considered an adequate explanation for the reported sufferings of voluntary isolates such as religious solitaries.

The length of time in isolation does not seem a satisfactory explanation, for in quite a few of these autobiographical reminiscences the reported peak of suffering occurs after only a few hours of isolation and in many of these reports the peak seems to occur within two or three days of isolation. Many other explanations are possible, of course, but the incompatibility of our case studies with the autobiographical reports can most reasonably be explained in terms of the biased sample of documents available for this sort of library survey. Certainly not everyone in isolation suffers so dramatically, and probably only those who have really undergone extreme suffering bother to write about the experience. Also, our own subjects were volunteers, and it is likely that only those who did not anticipate any difficulties would agree to take part in this study.

In any case the fact that we were unable to produce a state of social need or of even mild suffering with any consistency ruled out further research along this line. It had been our intention to conduct an experiment, eventually, in which the social needs would be manipulated by means of social deprivation and the effects of this manipulation noted on a variety of variables, such as influencibility, post-isolation social behavior, and so on. The results of these few cases made it quite clear that this would not be an easy experiment to carry out. It seemed evident that it would require some ten to fourteen days of isolation to produce the state of social need required, that in the process the very best subjects would be lost, and that to complete the multi-condition experiment planned would, with the facilities available, require approximately eleven years.

Needless to say, it was with considerable relief that this particular experiment was abandoned. Happily, however, this was not all wasted effort, for it did lead directly into a more promising line of investigation on the nature of the variables affecting the affiliative tendency.

2

*A*nxiety and *A*ffiliation

One of the consequences of isolation appears to be a psychological state which in its extreme form resembles a full-blown anxiety attack. In many of the autobiographical reports and in the interview protocol of our single subject who demanded his release after only two hours of confinement, there are strong indications of an overwhelming nervousness, of tremendous suffering and pain, and of a general "going-to-pieces." A milder form is illustrated by the two of our five subjects who reported that they had felt jittery, tense, and uneasy. At the other extreme, two subjects went through the experience with complete aplomb and reported no difficulties. The whole range of reactions is represented, and though we have little idea as to the variables which determine whether the reaction to isolation will be equanimity or terror, it is evident that anxiety, in some degree, is a fairly common concomitant of isolation. For a variety of frankly intuitive reasons, it seemed reasonable to expect that if conditions of isolation produce anxiety, conditions of anxiety would lead to the increase of affiliative tendencies. In order to test this proposition the following very simple experiment was constructed.

EXPERIMENTAL PROCEDURE

There were two experimental conditions, one of high anxiety and one of low anxiety. Anxiety was manipulated in the following fashion. In the high-anxiety condition, the subjects, all college girls, strangers to one another, entered a room to find facing them a gentleman of serious mien, horn-rimmed glasses, dressed in a white laboratory coat, stethoscope dribbling out of his pocket, behind him an array of formidable electrical junk. After a few preliminaries, the experimenter began:

Allow me to introduce myself, I am Dr. Gregor Zilstein of the Medical School's Departments of Neurology and Psychiatry. I have asked you all to come today in order to serve as subjects in an experiment concerned with the effects of electrical shock.

Zilstein paused ominously, then continued with a seven- or eight-minute recital of the importance of research in this area, citing electroshock therapy, the increasing number of accidents due to electricity, and so on. He concluded in this vein:

What we will ask each of you to do is very simple. We would like to give each of you a series of electric shocks. Now, I feel I must be completely honest with you and tell you exactly what you are in for. These shocks will hurt, they will be painful. As you can guess, if, in research of this sort, we're to learn anything at all that will really help humanity, it is necessary that our shocks be intense. What we will do is put an electrode on your hand, hook you into apparatus such as this [Zilstein points to the electrical-looking gadgetry behind him], give you a series of electric shocks, and take various measures such as your pulse rate, blood pressure, and so on. Again, I do want to be honest with you and tell you that these shocks will be quite painful but, of course, they will do no permanent damage.

In the low-anxiety condition, the setting and costume were precisely the same except that there was no electrical apparatus in the room. After introducing himself, Zilstein proceeded:

I have asked you all to come today in order to serve as subjects in an experiment concerned with the effects of electric shock. I hasten to add, do not let the word "shock" trouble you; I am sure that you will enjoy the experiment.

Then precisely the same recital on the importance of the research, concluding with:

What we will ask each one of you to do is very simple. We would like to give each of you a series of very mild electric shocks. I assure you that what you will feel will not in any way be painful. It will resemble more a tickle or a tingle than anything unpleasant. We will put an electrode on your hand, give you a series of very mild shocks and measure such things as your pulse rate and blood pressure, measures with which I'm sure you are all familiar from visits to your family doctor.

From this point on, the experimental procedures in the two conditions were identical. In order to get a first measurement of the effectiveness of the anxiety manipulation, the experimenter continued:

Before we begin, I'd like to have you tell us how you feel about taking part in this experiment and being shocked. We need this information in order to fully understand your reactions in the shocking apparatus. I ask you therefore to be as honest as possible in answering and describe your feelings as accurately as possible.

He then passed out a sheet headed, "How do you feel about being shocked?" and asked the subjects to check the appropriate point on a five-point scale ranging from "I dislike the idea very much" to "I enjoy the idea very much."*

This done, the experimenter continued:

Before we begin with the shocking proper there will be about a ten-minute delay while we get this room in order. We have several pieces of equipment to bring in and get set up. With this many people in the room, this would be very difficult to do, so we will have to ask you to be kind enough to leave the room.

Here is what we will ask you to do for this ten-minute period of waiting. We have on this floor a number of additional rooms, so that each of you, if you would like, can wait alone in your own room. These rooms are comfortable and

---

* The reader may well feel that this is hardly the most appropriate scale for measuring degree of anxiety. In experiments to be described in later chapters, precisely the same anxiety manipulation was employed and a scale that more directly tapped the anxiety dimension was added. This scale correlated with the "dislike-enjoy" scale described above with $r = +.76$.

spacious; they all have armchairs, and there are books and magazines in each room. It did occur to us, however, that some of you might want to wait for these ten minutes together with some of the other girls here. If you would prefer this, of course, just let us know. We'll take one of the empty class-rooms on this floor and you can wait together with some of the other girls there.

The experimenter then passed out a sheet on which the sub-jects could indicate their preference. This sheet read as follows:

Please indicate below whether you prefer waiting your turn to be shocked alone or in the company of others.
————I prefer being alone.
————I prefer being with others.
————I really don't care.

In order to get a measure of the intensity of the subjects' de-sires to be alone or together, the experimenter continued:

With a group this size and with the number of additional rooms we have, it's not always possible to give each girl exactly what she'd like. So be perfectly honest and let us know how much you'd like to be alone or together with other girls. Let us know just how you feel, and we'll use that information to come as close as possible to putting you into the arrangement of your choice.

The experimenter then passed out the following scale:

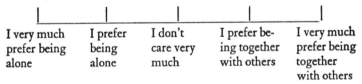

| I very much prefer being alone | I prefer being alone | I don't care very much | I prefer be-ing together with others | I very much prefer being together with others |

To get a final measure of the effectiveness of the anxiety manipu-lation, the experimenter continued:

It has, of course, occurred to us that some of you may not wish to take part in this experiment. Now, we would find it per-fectly understandable if some of you should feel that you do not want to be a subject in an experiment in which you will be shocked. If this is the case just let us know. I'll pass out this sheet on which you may indicate whether or not you want to go on. If you do wish to be a subject, check "yes"; if you do not wish to take part, check "no" and you may leave. Of course, if you check "no" we cannot give you credit in your psychology classes for having taken part in this experiment.

After the subjects had marked their sheets, the experiment was over and the experimenter took off his white coat and explained in detail the purpose of the experiment and the reasons for the various deceptions practiced. The cooperation of the subjects was of course enlisted in not talking about the experiment to other students.

In summary, in this experimental set-up, anxiety has been manipulated by varying the fear of being shocked. The affiliative tendency is measured by the subject's preference for "Alone," "Together," or "Don't care" and by the expressed intensity of this preference.

SUBJECTS

The subjects in this study were all girls, students in Introductory Psychology courses at the University of Minnesota. At the beginning of each semester, students in these classes may sign up for a subject pool. More than 90 percent of the students usually do so, for they receive one additional point on their final examination for each experimental hour they serve. This fact should be kept in mind when considering the proportion of subjects who refused to continue in the experiment.

The experimental sessions were run with groups of five to eight girls at a time, for a total of 32 subjects in the high-anxiety condition and 30 subjects in the low-anxiety condition. A deliberate attempt was made to insure that the subjects did not know one another before coming to the experiment. Despite our best efforts, 16 percent of the subjects had known one another beforehand. Data for these subjects were discarded, for it seemed clear that previous friendship would thoroughly confound the meaning of a choice of "Together" or "Alone." It should be noted, however, that though in both conditions such girls chose "Together" considerably more often than did girls who had not known one another before the experiment, the between-condition differences were in the same direction for both groups of subjects.

On this same point, an attempt was made to prevent the subjects from talking to one another while waiting for the experiment to begin, for again it was felt that an interesting conversation or a particularly friendly girl might confound the choice of "Together" or "Alone." As each subject entered the experimental room, she was handed a multipaged questionnaire labeled "Biographical Inventory" and asked to begin filling it out. This device worked well and effectively prevented any chatter until all of the subjects had arrived and the experimenter could begin his monologue.

RESULTS

Table 1 presents data permitting evaluation of the effectiveness of the manipulation of anxiety. The column labeled "Anx" presents the mean score, by condition, of responses to the question "How do you feel about being shocked?" The greater the score, the greater the anxiety; a score greater than 3 indicates dislike. Clearly there are large and significant differences between the two conditions.

TABLE 1

EFFECTIVENESS OF THE ANXIETY MANIPULATION

	N	Anx	% S's refusing to continue
Hi Anx	32	3.69	18.8
Lo Anx	30	2.48	0
		$t = 5.22$	Exact $p = .03$
		$p^* < .001$	

* The probability values reported throughout this volume are all based on two-tailed tests of significance.

The results of the second measure of anxiety, a subject's willingness to continue in the experiment when given the opportunity to drop out, are presented in the column labeled "% S's refusing to continue." This is, perhaps, the best single indicator of the effectiveness of the manipulation, for it is a reality-bound measure. Again it is clear that the manipulation of anxiety has been successful. Some 19 percent of subjects in the high-anxiety condition refused to continue in the experiment. All subjects in the low-anxiety condition were willing to go through with the experiment.

The effect of anxiety on the affiliative tendency may be noted in Table 2, where, for each condition, the number of subjects choosing "Together," "Alone," or "Don't Care" is tabulated. It is evident that there is a strong positive relationship between anxiety and the index of affiliative tendency, the proportion of subjects choosing the "Together" alternative. Some 63 percent of subjects in the high-anxiety condition wanted to be together with other subjects while they waited to be shocked. In the low-anxiety condition only 33 percent of the subjects wished to be together.

TABLE 2

RELATIONSHIP OF ANXIETY TO THE AFFILIATIVE TENDENCY

	No. Choosing			Overall Intensity
	Together	*Don't Care*	*Alone*	
Hi Anx	20	9	3	+.88
Lo Anx	10	18	2	+.35
	$X^2_{Tog \text{ vs } DC + A} = 5.27$			$t = 2.83$
	$.02 < p < .05$			$p < .01$

The column labeled "Overall Intensity" in Table 2 presents the mean score for all subjects, in each condition, of responses to the scale designed to measure the intensity of the desire to be alone or together with others. The point "I don't care very much" is scored as zero. The two points on this scale indicating a preference for being together with other subjects are scored as $+1$ and $+2$ respectively. The points indicating a preference for being alone are scored as -1 and -2. The mean scores of this scale provide the best overall index of the magnitude of affiliative desires, for this score combines choice and intensity of choice. Also, this index incorporates the relatively milder preferences of subjects who chose the "Don't Care" alternative, for 30 percent of these subjects did express some preference on this scale. Again it is clear that affiliative desires increase with anxiety. The mean intensity score for high-anxiety subjects is $+.88$ and for low-anxiety subjects is $+.35$.

Expectations, then, are confirmed, but confirmed, in truth, in a blaze of ambiguity, for the several terms of the formulation "anxiety leads to the arousal of affiliative tendencies" are still vague. What is meant by the "affiliative tendency," and precisely why do the subjects choose to be together when anxious? What is meant by "anxiety," and what are the limits of this relationship? What is meant by "leads to," and, historically, just how and why is this relationship established? The remainder of this monograph is devoted to consideration of these questions and to a description of research designed to clarify and elaborate the nature of this relationship.

3

The Affiliative Tendency—Directionality

Anxiety leads to the arousal of affiliative tendencies—but why? What specific needs are aroused by this manipulation of anxiety? What satisfactions are sought in the company of other people? So many explanations of the anxiety-affiliation relationship are possible that let us proceed by asking a question which will permit us to begin discriminating among possible alternative formulations of this relationship. Is the choice of "Together" a discriminating choice or not? That is, does this choice represent a desire to be with people in general, *any* kind of people; or is it a desire to be with people of a certain kind—in this case people who are in a similar situation? In the experiment described, it is impossible to make this distinction, for if a subject chose "Together," she was necessarily choosing to be with people in a similar plight. Yet this question is of primary importance in the interpretation of this experiment, for one would seek to account for the anxiety-affiliation relationship along entirely different theoretical lines, depending upon whether the affiliative choice was general or directional. Should the choice of "Together" prove to be general, it would point our investigations and formulation toward a sort of generalized need for affiliation. If the choice of "Together" is directional, one would search for more specific needs whose satisfaction requires the presence of others in a similar plight. In order to settle the issue of directionality the following experiment was conducted.

PROCEDURE

There were two experimental conditions, in both of which subjects were run one at a time instead of in the group setting employed in the previous experiment. Again, the subjects were all girls, undergraduates who received extra credit in their psychology courses for taking part in the experiment. In most other respects the experimental procedure in both conditions was identical with that used in the "Hi Anx" condition described in Chapter 2—the same room with electrical apparatus strewn about, the same medical experimenter, and precisely the same patter about the importance of research on electric shock and the necessary painfulness of the shocks that would be administered. The same instruments were used to measure the degree of manipulated anxiety and to determine the desire to be alone or with others, although one measuring instrument was modified for this study. A new scale was substituted for the scale originally used to measure the intensity of a subject's desire to be alone or with others. The zero point was eliminated and the scale points read:

———I very much prefer being alone.	(-3)
———I prefer being alone.	(-2)
———I slightly prefer being alone.	(-1)
———I slightly prefer being together with others.	$(+1)$
———I prefer being together with others.	$(+2)$
———I very much prefer being together with others.	$(+3)$

The figures in parentheses represent the values used in scoring this scale.

The two conditions differed in only a single respect. In one condition, to be called the "Same State" condition, immediately after the experimenter had indicated that there would be about a ten-minute delay before the experiment could begin, he continued:

Here, then, is what we will ask you to do for this ten-minute period of waiting. We have on this floor another room, so that, if you'd like, you may wait alone. This room is comfortable and spacious, it has an armchair and there are books and the latest magazines in the room. It did occur to us, however, that you might prefer waiting together with some other people. If this is the case we do have an alternative for you. At the present time some of my assistants are talking to other girls who will be taking part in this same experiment. If you would prefer to wait together with some other girls we have a waiting room down the hall in which you may wait together with some of these girls.

In the second condition, to be called the "Different State" condition, after describing the "Alone" room, the experimenter continued:

It did occur to us, however, that you might prefer waiting together with some other people. If this is the case we do have an alternative for you. There is a waiting room down the hall in which there are other girls waiting to talk to their professors and advisors. If you would prefer, you may wait there.

In the "Same State" condition, then, the subjects have a choice of being alone or being with other girls who are, presumably, undergoing exactly the same experience. In the "Different State" condition, the subjects have a choice of being alone or being with other girls with whom, as far as the experiment goes, they have nothing in common. If the affiliative choice is general, so that anxious subjects want to be with anyone at all just so long as they are with *someone*, there should be no difference in the proportion of subjects who choose "Together" in the two conditions. If the affiliative choice is directional, the subjects in the "Same State" conditions should tend to choose "Together" more often than those in the "Different State" condition.

RESULTS

Before examining the distribution of "Alone" and "Together" choices in the two conditions, note the levels of manipulated anxiety in Table 3. The data recorded here are for the two anxiety measures described in Chapter 2. In addition to these twenty subjects, one girl in the "Same State" condition refused to continue in the experiment. She made this decision, however, before choosing among the "Alone," "Together," and "Don't Care" alternatives. Since these data on anxiety level are being presented only to allow evaluation of the comparability of subjects who made this choice, this single case is excluded from this table.

TABLE 3

LEVEL OF ANXIETY IN THE TWO EXPERIMENTAL CONDITIONS

	N	Anx	% S's refusing to continue
Same State	10	3.30	0
Different State	10	3.40	0
		$p = n.s.$	$p = n.s.$

Table 3 makes it immediately clear that there are no differences in anxiety between the two conditions. On both measures, the scores are almost identical for the two groups of subjects. Any differences in affiliative choice pattern cannot, then, be attributed to differential anxiety.

Parenthetically, it might be noted that though the anxiety-producing instructions were precisely the same as those used in the high-anxiety condition described earlier, these anxiety scores are noticeably lower than corresponding scores in the previous experiment. (See Table 1.) This difference in the effectiveness of the high-anxiety manipulation seems most clearly attributable to differential rapport between experimenter and subject. Despite the experimenter's deliberate attempt to behave identically in both experiments, inevitably a more personal relationship resulted in the two-person experiment. In this two-person study, the subjects felt free to ask questions and make comments and frequently did so, resulting in a relationship more informal than in the group setting, where almost no subject seemed to feel uninhibited enough to comment freely.

The effect of these manipulations on the pattern of affiliative choice is presented in Table 4, where for each condition the number of subjects choosing each of the alternatives is tallied. It is

TABLE 4

DIRECTIONALITY AND THE AFFILIATIVE TENDENCY

	No. Choosing			Overall Intensity
	To-gether	Don't Care	Alone	
Same State	6	4	0	$+1.40$
Different State	0	10	0	$-.20$

$$t = 4.93$$
Exact p_{Tog} vs $_{DC + A} = .01$ $p < .001$

evident that the affiliative choice is highly directional. In the "Same State" condition, where a subject has the opportunity to be with other subjects in the experiment, six of ten subjects chose the "Together" alternative. In the "Different State" condition, where a choice of "Together" would allow the subjects to be with people who have nothing to do with the experiment, none of the ten subjects chose "Together." On the overall intensity scale, the difference between the two conditions is huge. It will be recalled that this is a scale designed to measure the intensity of a subject's desire to be alone or with others. It should be noted in Table 4 that a mean minus score is recorded for the "Different State" condition. Subjects somewhat preferred being alone to being with people who had nothing to do with the experiment.

Plainly, then, under conditions of anxiety the affiliative tendency is highly directional—an experimental finding which removes one shred of ambiguity from the old saw "Misery loves company." Misery doesn't love just any kind of company, it loves only miserable company. Whatever the needs aroused by the manipulation of anxiety, it would seem that their satisfaction demands the presence of others in a similar situation.

4

The Affiliative Tendency—Communication

Though the results of the experiment on directionality remove one major ambiguity from the interpretation of the anxiety-affiliation relationship, the choice of "Together" must still be viewed as a complex affair. When anxious, people may wish to be with others in a similar plight for any of a still large variety of reasons, and it is clear that if we are to understand the nature of this relationship it will be necessary to evaluate alternative explanations for the choice of "Together." As a first step toward such evaluation, the following is suggested as a reasonable list of explanatory possibilities for why anxious subjects chose to be together more often than non-anxious subjects.

Escape. Subjects may have wanted to be together as a way of getting out of the experiment. It is conceivable that during the experiment proper the girls may have been reluctant to interrupt the proceedings and openly admit that they were afraid and did not want to be shocked. (In the experiment described, the subjects were allowed to decide whether or not they wished to continue in the experiment. However, they were given this choice only *after* they had indicated a preference for "Together," "Alone," or "Don't Care.") It is possible, then, that subjects may have chosen "Together" in the hope of talking others out of taking part in the experiment and, better still, allowing themselves to be talked out of participating.

Cognitive Clarity. In the introductory chapter, we have cited studies which indicate that in ambiguous or novel situations forces arise that impel people to associate with other people as a means of achieving some degree of clarity about an otherwise incomprehensible event. The experimental situation was completely unexpected and, in all likelihood, unique in the subjects' experiences. It is conceivable, then, that subjects chose to be together in the hope of being able to talk about the experiment and get a better idea as to what the whole thing was about. And, since the high-anxiety instructions were undoubtedly more dramatic and novel, needs for cognitive clarity may have been greater in this condition than in the low-anxiety condition.

Direct Anxiety Reduction. People do serve a direct anxiety-reducing function for one another. They comfort and support, they reassure one another and attempt to bolster courage. Since anxiety is undoubtedly an unpleasant state, it is possible that highly anxious subjects chose "Together" as a means toward this sort of social reassurance and toward reducing anxiety.

Indirect Anxiety Reduction. One of the most effective devices for anxiety reduction is simply "to get one's mind off one's troubles." Movies, television, and mystery stories are devices that elegantly serve as this diverting function. And people, of course, can be the best of diverters, for not only may they be more entertaining and distracting, but also they can effectively compel attention more than most other distractors. Conceivably, then, highly anxious subjects chose "Together" in the hope that being with others might more effectively distract them than being alone with their worries and a few magazines.

Self-Evaluation. Just as one compares himself to other people as a means of establishing a framework and social reality for his opinions, so one may use other people to evaluate his emotions and feelings. In a novel, emotion-producing situation, unless the situation is completely clear-cut the feelings one experiences or "should" experience may not be easily interpretable, and it may require some degree of social interaction and comparison to appropriately label and identify a feeling. We are suggesting, of course, that the emotions are highly susceptible to social influence and that, as has been suggested for the opinions, a need for social evaluation of the emotions may be active. Needless to say, this point demands elaboration, and in a more appropriate section of this volume we shall elaborate.

One could, of course, consider self evaluation as a special case of "cognitive clarity" as used above. For the moment, however, we would prefer to keep these two categories distinct, with cognitive clarity referring strictly to information gathering of the order of gossip or newspaper reading and self evaluation referring to the attempt via social comparison processes to place and evaluate one's own opinions and feelings.

Almost all of these alternative explanations have a plausible ring, and it is conceivable that the experimental results might be explained by any or all of these alternatives. To understand these data fully, then, it is necessary to attempt to partial out the effects of these several alternatives. The results of the directionality experiment would already indicate that "indirect anxiety reduction" is not an appropriate explanation of the anxiety–affiliation relationship. If this diverting function played any major role in determining the choice of "Together," there should have been a higher proportion of "Together" choices in the "Different" than in the "Same State" condition of the directionality experiment, for, certainly, people having nothing to do with the experiment should have been more effective diverters than other subjects in the experiment. The results, of course, are quite the opposite of this expectation.

In order to evaluate the importance of the remaining alternatives, let us consider the differential implications for these several explanations of a dimension which we will call "the opportunity to communicate." Either to escape from the situation or to satisfy one's curiosity and achieve some degree of cognitive clarity requires the opportunity to talk to one's fellow subjects. On the other hand, verbal communication, though certainly helpful, is probably not indispensable for either self evaluation or anxiety reduction. An exchange of sympathetic glances or a friendly pat on the back may indeed be anxiety reducing. Similarly, no great perspicacity is required to surmise, just by looking, the reactions of people to anxiety-provoking situations, and a glance may tell a good deal about how other members of an experimental group are reacting as compared with oneself. The experimental manipulation of the opportunity to communicate should, then, permit further paring down of alternative interpretations of the relationship at issue. To this end, an experiment was performed which systematically restricted communication possibilities.

The experiment conducted was in its essential features identical with the initial experiment described in Chapter 2—again the same setting, precisely the same manipulation of anxiety administered to groups of five to eight female subjects, essentially the same measures of affiliative desires. This experiment differed from the original, however, in the description of the "Together" alternative.

In two conditions, a high- and a low-anxiety condition, when the subjects were presented with the choice of "Together," "Alone," or "Don't Care," they were in addition told:

> Before you make your choice I'd like to request one favor of you. I'd like to ask you, please, when you leave this room and while you're waiting for the experiment to begin, not to talk about this experiment or electric shock. You can, of course, talk about anything else you'd like, but until this experiment is over I must ask you not to talk to one another about anything relating to this experiment. Will that be O.K.?

The experimenter then waited until he had a nod of agreement from everyone before continuing. Conditions in which these instructions were used will be called "Irrelevant-Talk" conditions.

These instructions, of course, are intended to partial out the effects of those alternatives requiring the opportunity to discuss the experiment from the effects of the remaining possible explanations. The "escape" and "cognitive clarity" alternatives can be operative only if there is the opportunity to talk about the experiment or about one's reactions to being shocked.

In a second set of conditions, to be called "No-Talk" conditions, before the subjects could choose among "Together," "Alone," and "Don't Care," they were told:

Before you make your choice, I'd like to request one favor of you. I'd like to ask you, please, when you leave this room, and while you're waiting for the experiment to begin, not to talk to one another. You can, of course, read or do anything else you like, but I must ask you not to talk, not to exchange a single word with one another. Will that be O.K.?

Again, the experimenter waited for nods of agreement before continuing.

These instructions, then, permit direct examination of the effects of those explanations for which verbal communication is not absolutely required. Though, certainly, anxiety reduction and self evaluation are facilitated by direct discussion, verbal communication is by no means indispensable for the satisfaction of these needs. Presumably, then, if such needs are strongly operative there should be a positive relationship between anxiety and the affiliative tendency even when no talking is permitted. Finally, a comparison of these two sets of conditions should permit an additional check on the importance of the "indirect anxiety reduction" explanation, for such a factor could be operating in the "Irrel-Talk" conditions but hardly at all in the "No-Talk" conditions.

In order to make sure that the subjects had listened to and understood the instructions restricting communication, all of the subjects were asked to check a brief questionnaire administered immediately before the announcement that the experiment was over and before explanations of the hoax were offered. The experimenter explained that he was interested in learning how clear his instructions on this point had been and after a brief introduction asked the subjects to choose among the following alternatives.*

———You could talk to the others about anything at all.
———You could talk to the others about anything except the experiment or electric shock.
———You could not say a single word to the others.

* Though this check list allows evaluation of the subjects' understanding of these instructions, it of course indicates nothing about a

Only four subjects failed to understand the instructions. These few cases, of course, are eliminated from the analysis.

To summarize, there were four experimental conditions:

> High Anxiety–Irrelevant Talk (to be abbreviated Hi Irrel)
> Low Anxiety–Irrelevant Talk (to be abbreviated Lo Irrel)
> High Anxiety–No-Talk (to be abbreviated Hi No-Talk)
> Low Anxiety–No-Talk (to be abbreviated Lo No-Talk)

The major difference, then, between these conditions and the original experiment is in the description of the "Together" alternative. In the original experiment, no restrictions were placed on the "Together" alternative and the subjects assumed that they could talk about anything they liked if they chose "Together." In "Irrelevant" conditions, restrictions were placed on the content of communication; in "No-Talk" conditions, there was a prohibition against any communication at all. In addition to these deliberate variations, circumstances or second thoughts forced the following procedural modifications.

1. A different experimenter conducted the experimental sessions for these four conditions. The original experimenter had been a gentleman of 35 who looked 40; the new experimenter was 25 years old and looked it. With only the most trivial variations, however, the two experimenters used precisely the same patter.

2. In the original experiment, the subjects had all been taken from the Introductory Psychology class subject pool and received extra credit in their course work for serving as subjects. In the "Irrel No-Talk" experiment there were simply not enough girls in the subject pool to satisfy the needs of the experiment, and it was necessary to recruit additional subjects from introductory

---

subject's intention to follow the instructions. An experiment conducted by Wrightsman (59), however, indicates that subjects do take such instructions seriously. In one of Wrightsman's conditions precisely these same "No-Talk" instructions were used and the subjects were then actually left together for five minutes. In none of seventeen such experimental groups was there a violation of the prohibition against talk.

courses in sociology, education, and political science. These volunteers received no class credit for taking part in the experiment, and it will of course be necessary to take account of this fact in evaluating the effectiveness of the anxiety manipulation.

3. A new measure of anxiety was added. This measure was administered at the same time and with the same words as the earlier described "Dislike-Enjoy" scale. The new scale read:

How nervous or uneasy do you feel about taking part in this experiment and being shocked?

I feel extremely uneasy	I feel very uneasy	I feel quite uneasy	I feel a little uneasy	I feel relatively calm	I feel completely calm
(6)	(5)	(4)	(3)	(2)	(1)

4. The scale used to measure the intensity of a subject's desire to be alone or with others was the scale described on page 21.

5. The description of the physical surroundings for those who chose "Together" was modified. In the original experiment, the experimenter had said:

Each of you, if you would like, can wait alone in your own room. These rooms are comfortable and spacious; they all have armchairs, and there are books and magazines in each room. It did occur to us, however, that some of you might want to wait for these ten minutes together with some of the other girls here. If you would prefer this, of course, just let us know. We'll take one of the empty classrooms on this floor and you can wait together with some of the other girls there.

In trial runs of the "No-Talk" condition, the idea of sitting around an empty classroom and saying nothing at all, simply staring at one another, seemed quite silly to both the experimenter and the subjects and the instructions were consequently changed to:

Each of you, if you would like, can wait alone in your own room. These rooms are comfortable and spacious; they all have armchairs, and there are books and magazines in each room. It did occur to us, however, that some of you might want to wait for these ten minutes together with some of the other girls here. If you would prefer this, just let us know, and we'll put those of you who want to wait together in the same room.

It would have been obviously desirable to have left these particular instructions unchanged. Since in their original form, however, they seemed to disturb the mood of serious and sober consideration of the alternatives, it seemed wisest to modify these instructions to the form described and this new form was used in both the "No-Talk" and "Irrel" conditions. It is a reasonable guess, however, that these modifications have affected the valence or desirability of the "Together" alternative, for "Together" now includes books, magazines, and armchairs rather than merely an empty classroom, as before. In addition, in the original instructions there is some implication of extra trouble for the experimenter if someone chose "Together," whereas there is no such implication in the modified instructions.

6. At the conclusion of the experiment, immediately after the subjects had answered the question designed to determine whether or not they had understood the instructions restricting communication, they were each handed a sheet of paper and asked to "try to think back to what went through your mind when you were deciding among 'Together,' 'Alone,' and 'Don't Care,' and, as well as you can, write down what it was that made you decide as you did."

RESULTS

In order to simplify presentation and discussion, the results of the "Irrel-Talk" and "No-Talk" conditions will be presented separately. In Table 5 are data on the effectiveness of the anxiety manipulation in the "Irrel-Talk" conditions. Under the heading "Anx 1" are listed mean scores on the "dislike-enjoy" scale described in previous chapters. Under the heading of "Anx 2" are listed mean scores on the "uneasy-calm" scale described earlier in this chapter. It is clear that on both of these scales there are large

TABLE 5

EFFECTIVENESS OF THE ANXIETY MANIPULATION IN THE
IRRELEVANT-TALK CONDITION

	N	Anx 1	Anx 2	% S's re-fusing to continue
Hi Irrel	44	3.51	3.32	11.4
Lo Irrel	42	2.41	2.35	2.4
		$t = 5.88$	$t = 4.06$	*Exact Test*
		$p < .001$	$p < .001$	$p = n.s.$

and significant differences between conditions. On the final measure of anxiety, willingness to continue in the experiment, the results are not as clear-cut. Some 11 percent of high-anxiety subjects refused to continue in the experiment and 2 percent of low-anxiety subjects refused to continue—a nonsignificant difference. Apparently the manipulation of anxiety had affected the subjects' general apprehensiveness but not sufficiently to affect strongly their decision as to whether or not to continue in the experiment. This becomes even clearer when the data for only those subjects who received class credit for taking part in this experiment is examined. Slightly less than 6 percent of these subjects refused to continue. When this figure is compared with the 19 percent of similar subjects in the original experiment (Table 1) who refused to continue, it becomes clear that the manipulation of high anxiety in the "Irrel-Talk" condition was not quite as effective as the same manipulation in the earlier experiment.

The effects of the anxiety manipulation on the affiliative tendency are recorded in Table 6. It is evident that there is little difference between the two conditions. Some 47 percent of "Hi Irrel" subjects chose "Together" as compared with 43 percent of "Lo Irrel" subjects. On the overall intensity measure there is only the slightest difference between the two conditions. A variety of interpretive alternatives is possible. It may be that anxiety is related

TABLE 6

RELATIONSHIP OF ANXIETY TO THE AFFILIATIVE TENDENCY
IN THE IRRELEVANT-TALK CONDITION*

	No. Choosing			
	To-gether	Don't Care	Alone	Overall Intensity
Hi Irrel	20	20	3	+1.07
Lo Irrel	18	22	2	+1.00
		$p = n.s.$		$p = n.s.$

* There is one fewer subject in the Hi Irrel condition than in this condition in Table 3. One subject was so determined not to take part in the experiment that she refused to indicate any preference.

to the affiliative tendency only under conditions of unrestricted communication; it may be that the relative weakness of the high-anxiety manipulation is responsible; or it may be that these results are a function of specific and still unlabeled characteristics of these subjects, a matter that has not yet been discussed but to which considerable attention will be devoted in ensuing chapters. The point at stake, of course, is basic to the interpretation of the relationship under consideration, and in order to provide further insight into these data it seemed advisable to undertake an internal analysis; that is, to compare the responses of truly anxious subjects with those of relatively calm subjects. If, under these conditions of restricted communication, there really is no relationship between anxiety and the affiliative tendency, there should be no difference between these two groups of subjects. If such a comparison does reveal differences between these two groups of subjects one could, at this point, very tentatively conclude that even under conditions of restricted communication there is a relationship between anxiety and affiliation and that either the relative weakness of the "Hi Anx" manipulation or the operation of still unspecified factors has obscured the differences between conditions.

The category "Truly Anxious" will include all subjects who

refused to continue in the experiment and all subjects who checked the two extreme dislike points on the Anx 1 scale. All other subjects who on this scale checked points indicating that they were indifferent to being shocked or enjoyed the idea of being shocked were categorized as "True Low Anxiety." The Anx 1 scale, rather than the Anx 2 scale, is used to distinguish between these groups only because in later analyses it will be necessary to make these breakdowns for subjects in the original experiment in which only the Anx 1 scale was administered. It should be pointed out again that these two scales correlate with $r = +.76$ and that in all of the comparisons to be made, it makes virtually no difference in the direction and magnitude of obtained differences which of these two scales is used to distinguish between truly high and low anxiety subjects.

The results of this internal analysis are presented in Table 7. Of the 29 subjects categorized "True Hi Irrel," 86 percent are from the manipulated "Hi Irrel" condition. Of the 56 subjects categorized "True Lo Irrel," 68 percent are from the manipulated "Lo Irrel" condition. It is evident from Table 7 that the relationship between anxiety and the affiliative tendency is again positive. Some 59 percent of all anxious subjects chose "Together" as compared with the 38 percent of non-anxious subjects who did so. On the overall intensity index, there are marked differences between the

TABLE 7

RELATIONSHIP OF ANXIETY TO THE AFFILIATIVE TENDENCY IN THE IRRELEVANT-TALK CONDITION (INTERNAL ANALYSIS)

	No. Choosing			Overall Intensity
	To-gether	Don't Care	Alone	
True Hi Irrel	17	11	1	$+1.48$
True Lo Irrel	21	31	4	$+ .80$
	$X^2_{Tog \; vs \; DC \, + \, A} = 3.44$			$t = 2.82$
	$.05 < p < .10$			$p = .01$

two groups. Tentatively, then, it would appear that even when it is impossible for the subjects to discuss anything relevant to their anxieties, anxious subjects want to be with others more than do calm subjects.

For the "No-Talk" conditions, data on the effectiveness of the manipulations are presented in Table 8, where it can be seen that all measures indicate that the high-anxiety manipulation has succeeded in provoking considerably more anxiety than the low-anxiety manipulation. On both scales there are large differences between the two conditions; on the measure of willingness to continue in the experiment, 24 percent of all high-anxiety subjects refused to continue, compared with 3 percent of low-anxiety subjects.

TABLE 8

EFFECTIVENESS OF THE ANXIETY MANIPULATION
IN THE NO-TALK CONDITIONS

	N	Anx 1	Anx 2	% S's re-fusing to continue
Hi No-Talk	37	3.80	4.05	24.3
Lo No-Talk	32	2.63	2.44	3.1
		$t = 5.85$	$t = 5.72$	*Exact Test*
		$p < .001$	$p < .001$	$p = .02$

The effects of anxiety on the affiliative tendencies of subjects in the "No Talk" conditions can be seen in Table 9, where it is apparent that there tends again to be a positive relationship between anxiety and the affiliative tendency but that the obtained differences are rather weak. In the high-anxiety condition, 40 percent of the subjects chose "Together" and in low-anxiety conditions 31 percent of the subjects did so. There are somewhat more substantial indications of a difference on the overall intensity measure, but this difference is significant at only the .08 level of confidence. These data, then, are consistent with previously dis-

TABLE 9

RELATIONSHIP OF ANXIETY TO THE AFFIRMATIVE TENDENCY
IN THE NO-TALK CONDITIONS*

	No. Choosing			
	To-gether	*Don't Care*	*Alone*	*Overall Intensity*
Hi No-Talk	14	20	1	+1.09
Lo No-Talk	10	19	3	+ .63
		p = n.s.		*t = 1.75*
				p = .08

* Two subjects were so determined not to take part in the experiment that they refused to indicate any preference. There are therefore two fewer subjects in Table 9 than in Table 8.

cussed results, but the magnitude of the obtained differences is such that no interpretive conclusion can leave us completely comfortable. Certainly there is every indication that the manipulation of anxiety has been successful in producing different levels of anxiety in the two experimental conditions. It may be, however, that with the restrictions placed on the "Together" situation, a strong positive relationship between anxiety and the affiliative tendency will manifest itself only when the severity and range of anxiety are greater than in the comparisons made, or, again, that other factors are obscuring between-condition differences. If these suppositions are correct, it might be expected that an internal analysis similar to that employed in the "Irrel-Talk" conditions would reveal a stronger relationship than is indicated in Table 9. The relevant data are presented in Table 10. Precisely the same criteria have been used to distinguish between "true" high- and low-anxiety subjects. Eighty-nine percent of those categorized "True Hi No-Talk" are from the manipulated "Hi No-Talk" condition; 73 percent of those classified "True Lo No-Talk" were subjects in the manipulated "Lo No-Talk" condition. It is immediately clear from this table that when the data are analyzed in

TABLE 10

RELATIONSHIP OF ANXIETY TO THE AFFILIATIVE TENDENCY IN THE
NO-TALK CONDITION (INTERNAL ANALYSIS)

	No. Choosing			
	To-gether	Don't Care	Alone	Overall Intensity
True Hi No-Talk	14	13	0	$+1.37$
True Lo No-Talk	10	26	4	$+ .50$
	$X^2{}_{Tog \, vs \, DC \, + \, A} = 5.05$			$t = 2.78$
	$.02 < p < .05$			$p < .01$

this fashion the relationship between anxiety and affiliation is considerably strengthened; 52 percent of the really anxious subjects chose "Together," 25 percent of the non-anxious subjects did so. On the intensity index there is a large difference between the two groups of subjects. The opportunity to communicate openly does not appear to be a necessary determinant of an anxious subject's desire to be with others.

To summarize experimental results so far, it would appear that anxiety is positively related to the affiliative tendency under conditions of free communication, under conditions of restricted communication, and under conditions where communication is impossible. At the moment, these conclusions must be considered tentative because of the reliance on internal analyses. We shall return to consideration of this rather intriguing pattern of weak between-condition differences and strong internal relationships in the following chapter. For the moment, let us consider the implications of this series of findings for the several alternative interpretations of the choice of "Together" under conditions of anxiety. The fact that it was necessary to modify the description of the "Together" alternative pretty much rules out any direct comparison of the results of the original experiment with the results of the "Irrel" and "No-Talk" conditions. It is still possible, however, to learn a considerable amount about these several alternatives from an analysis of the trends in the three conditions and a comparison of the "Irrel" and "No-Talk" conditions.

Firstly, one explanation of the results of the original experiment is the possibility that anxious subjects chose "Together" largely for "escape" reasons—that is, in the hope that they could convince other subjects and talk their own way out of the experiment. Though it is possible that a few subjects in the original study may have chosen "Together" for this reason, the fact that the relationship between anxiety and the affiliative tendency remains positive in both the "Irrel" and "No-Talk" conditions seems to rule out this factor as any sort of potent explanation, for to talk one's way out of the experiment requires that one be able to talk about the experiment. Though one might wish to argue that a truly frightened subject might have had no intention of abiding by these restrictions on communication, the existing data (see footnote on p. 29) indicate that this is simply not the case. In similar experiments where anxious subjects have actually waited together, they obey these instructions to the letter.

Further evidence on this point is available from the experiment by Wrightsman mentioned earlier. The experiment involved a manipulation of anxiety similar to that used in the experiments described so far. In one of Wrightsman's conditions, following the manipulation subjects were actually brought together, free to talk about anything they chose, for a five-minute period. In none of seventeen experimental groups did any subject, in any way, attempt to talk her way out of the experiment. It would certainly appear, then, that this "escape" motive is in no way a determinant of an anxious subject's choice of "Together."

Secondly, cognitive clarity or the need simply to get more information about what is going on also seems to be ruled out as any sort of potent motive by the results in the "Irrel" and "No-Talk" conditions. To get information about the experiment requires being able to talk about the experiment. Yet in both sets of conditions where such talk is ruled out the relationship between anxiety and the affiliative tendency remains positive.

Thirdly, the fact that the relationship between anxiety and affiliation is positive in the "No-Talk" conditions is a further indication that the "indirect anxiety reduction" (diverting oneself) explanation is not a particularly important determinant of these results, for such a factor would pretty much require the opportunity to talk. This factor, though, could still play some part in the results of the "Irrel-Talk" conditions, and comparison of the magnitude of the relationship in the two sets of conditions should indicate whether the presumed "indirect anxiety reduction" motive plays any part at all in this relationship. Some 58.6 percent of all true "Hi Anx Irrel" subjects chose "Together" as compared with 51.9 percent of true "Hi Anx No-Talk" subjects—a small and insignificant difference. The fact that the difference between the true "Lo Anx" subjects in these two conditions is of about the same order of magnitude (37.5 percent to 25.0 percent) would indicate that even this difference is due to variation in the attractiveness of the two sets of conditions rather than to any anxiety-reducing possibility that the opportunity to make irrelevant talk might afford.

Let us summarize the conclusions that may be drawn from this series of experiments which employ directionality and the opportunity to communicate as analytic devices for evaluating the power of alternative explanations of the relationship between anxiety and the affiliative tendency. Substantively it has been demonstrated that this relationship maintains itself under a range of conditions from complete freedom of communication to complete absence of verbal communication and that the relationship is highly directional and specific to people in similar plights. The interpretive implications of these findings have permitted considerable narrowing down of alternative interpretations of the relationship. The finding of directionality permits us to restrict our search for explanation to needs whose satisfaction requires the presence of others in a similar plight. The fact that the relationship remains positive under conditions of highly restricted communication permits exclusion of the "escape," the "cognitive clarity," and the "indirect anxiety reduction" explanations. Remaining are the "direct anxiety reduction" and "self evaluation" alternatives. Anxious subjects may choose "Together" as a means of reducing their own fears or as a social means of better understanding and evaluating their own feelings. A few fairly typical quotations from subjects in the "Hi Anx No-Talk" condition may serve to make these residual alternatives somewhat more vivid for the reader. In response to the post-experiment request to "write down what made you decide as you did," one subject wrote, "I wanted to wait with other people to see how they would react while waiting for the experiment. By seeing that they weren't worried then I wouldn't be." Certainly self-evaluative and possibly anxiety-reducing motives are evident in such a statement. And evaluative motives are implicit in the following quotation, "I thought that the others probably had the same feelings toward the experiment that I had, and this thought made me want to be with someone." Though such typical quotations helpfully put flesh on these abstractions, they cannot in themselves, even in numbers, be considered any sort of potent support for these residual alternatives. However, as the reader may have gratefully noted, such quotations are the very first *positive* sort of evidence offered in support of these residual interpretations of the anxiety-affiliation relationship. The experimental process of exclusion of alternatives, though necessary to a point, can never be completely satisfactory, for the interpretive usefulness of such a technique rests on the exhaustiveness of the list of alternatives. And, though we have fair confidence that our list has included the most plausible of possible explanations of the relationship between anxiety and the affiliative tendency, it will always be possible, of course, to suggest additional explanations which, though they may be far-fetched, cannot unequivocally be ruled out. In a later chapter experiments which directly test implications of the "direct anxiety reducing" and "self evaluative" explanations will be discussed. Our immediate concern, however, will involve an attempt to clarify the pattern of results revealed in the "Irrel" and "No-Talk" experiments—a pattern of weak between-condition differences and strong internal relationships.

5

Ordinal Position, Anxiety, and Affiliation—I

The experiments described in preceding chapters have revealed a consistent pattern. In those studies where anxiety has varied, there have been consistent indications of a positive relationship between anxiety and the affiliative tendency. However, where the initial experiment in this series revealed strong between-condition differences, subsequent experiments required internal analysis to demonstrate the relationship. In the discussion of the "Irrel" and "No-Talk" experiments it has been suggested that this pattern of results may stem from an insufficiently strong manipulation of anxiety, but this does not, after all, seem a particularly convincing explanation, for in the "Hi Anx No-Talk" condition, at least, indications are that anxiety was even greater than in the original experiment. It would appear, then, that we must search elsewhere to understand this particular pattern of results.

Experimental artifacts can sometimes account for such results, but since these several experiments were, with the minor modifications noted, almost identical, it is difficult to even guess what such artifacts might be. Sampling error could account for this pattern of results: if people who, for some systematic reason, were particularly prone to affiliate, were inadvertently to be overrepresented in a low-anxiety condition, precisely this pattern of results might be anticipated. But sampling of what? Along what dimension? Certainly there must be individual consistency in this sort of behavior. Some people habitually seek company when they feel anxious and troubled, while others customarily avoid people when they are disturbed. But how to distinguish such people? As a first approach to this problem, let us consider the genesis of the relationship—a consideration inevitably leading to a simple-minded learning formulation which, in its most elementary terms, would look something like this: baby, pin pricks baby, baby is scared, screams—mother hears scream, rushes to baby, investigates, removes pin, kisses sore spot, caresses, fondles, soothes, and so on. In short, people do serve as anxiety reducers for one another. Now if this sort of proposition amounts to anything, it should lead to something that could be tested, and it seemed plausible, at least, to suspect that in terms of our experimental variables there might be differences between first-born and later-born children. Considerations such as these might support this expectation:

First, with her first child, a mother is undoubtedly more ill at ease and more worried than she is with her later children. She probably responds to more signals, responds more quickly, stays longer, and generally does a more effective, all-around job of reducing anxiety with a first child than with later children. By the time she has her second or third child, besides having less time to pay attention she is certainly more blasé and sophisticated about the business of child rearing; and by the time she has had her fourth or fifth, she may simply be too worn out to care very much.

Second, younger children usually have threatening, anxiety-provoking persons in their immediate environment. By reputation, at least, older children get their exercise by knocking the younger ones about.

Though these considerations have a plausible ring to them, it should be made clear that we do not wish seriously to defend these particular arguments. They are offered at this point only in the hope of making modestly tenable, at least, the suggestion that ordinal position of birth affects the social nature of the response to anxiety. Without examining further the merit of these arguments, this general line of thought does lead to the expectation that under anxiety-provoking conditions first-born and only children will manifest stronger affiliative needs than later-born children. If this is true, it might be expected that in the preceding experiments subjects in high-anxiety conditions who are first-born or only children will choose "Together" relatively more often than subjects who are later-born. The relevant data are presented in Table 11. This table and the following similar tables are made up of four sub-tables. Sub-tables labeled *a, b,* and *c* present data for each of the three experimental conditions separately. Sub-table *d* presents the pooled data for all experimental conditions. Since in all of the major tables the trends are the same in each of the experimental conditions, we shall for simplicity's sake restrict discussion to the pooled data. The total *N* in each of these tables is slightly less than in tables in the preceding chapters. These small discrepancies are due to the elimination of all twins and adopted children from analyses of the effects of ordinal position.

TABLE 11

ORDINAL POSITION AND REACTIONS TO ANXIETY IN
HIGH-ANXIETY CONDITIONS

	a. Hi Anx—Original Experiment No. choosing		*b. Hi Irrel No. choosing*	
	To- gether	*Don't Care and Alone*	*To- gether*	*Don't Care and Alone*
First-born and only	12	5	12	6
Later-born	7	6	8	17
	c. Hi No-Talk No. choosing		*d. Pooled Hi Anx No. choosing*	
	To- gether	*Don't Care and Alone*	*To- gether*	*Don't Care and Alone*
First-born and only	8	5	32	16
Later-born	6	16	21	39

$$X^2 = 10.70$$
$$p < .01$$

In Table 11*d* it is quite clear that in the high-anxiety conditions first-born and only children strongly prefer being together, whereas later-born children do not. Some 67 percent of all first-born and only subjects chose "Together" and only 35 percent of later-born subjects did so.* Strong as these results are, their interpretation is ambiguous, for it is unclear whether these tendencies are specific to anxiety or simply indicate that first-born and only children are more sociable; that is, that under any condition first-born and only children might want to be with others more than would later-born children.

In order to choose between these alternatives it is necessary only to examine the data in Table 12, where the choices in low-anxiety conditions are recorded. In Table 12d it is evident that there is

TABLE 12

ORDINAL POSITION AND REACTIONS TO ANXIETY IN
LOW-ANXIETY CONDITIONS

	a. Lo Anx—Original Experiment No. choosing		b. Lo Irrel No. choosing	
	To-gether	Don't Care and Alone	To-gether	Don't Care and Alone
First-born and only	4	9	5	9
Later-born	6	10	12	15
	c. Lo No-Talk No. choosing		d. Pooled Lo Anx No. choosing	
	To-gether	Don't Care and Alone	To-gether	Don't Care and Alone
First-born and only	5	13	14	31
Later-born	5	8	23	33
			$X^2 = 1.19$	
			$p < .30$	

* In the experiment on directionality, only the "Same State" condition can be considered as roughly comparable in design to these three high-anxiety conditions. The results in this condition are completely consistent with the relationships noted here. There were two first-born subjects, both of whom chose "Together," and eight later-born subjects, of whom only four chose "Together."

no such tendency in low-anxiety conditions. If anything, the trend is slightly reversed, for 31 percent of first-born and only children chose "Together" and 41 percent of later-born subjects did so. Clearly, then, these results are specific to anxiety, and it may be concluded that anxiety produces considerably stronger manifestations of affiliative needs in first-born and only children than in later-born children.

In terms of the hypothesized relationship between anxiety and affiliation these results could be due to two factors. Either the level of manipulated anxiety is greater for first-born and only children or the link between anxiety and affiliation is stronger for first-born and only children, or both. Let us examine first the relationship of ordinal position to the degree of manipulated anxiety. In Table 13 are recorded, for high-anxiety conditions, data from all of the indices of anxiety. There are, again, substantial differences between first-born subjects and later-born subjects. On both scales of anxiety, first-born and only subjects indicate that they are considerably more nervous than later-born subjects. On the measure of willingness to go through with the experiment and be shocked, 28 percent of all first-born and only subjects refused to continue in the experiment and only 8 percent of all later-born subjects were unwilling to continue. Clearly, then, anxiety-provoking situations arouse considerably more anxiety and fear in early-born children than in later-born children.

In low-anxiety conditions there is no reason to expect any particular differences in ordinal positions, for in these experimental conditions there is nothing of which to be afraid. At most, it might be expected that a very few subjects would overreact to the experimental situation, in which case it should be anticipated that first-borns would have slightly higher mean anxiety scores than later-borns. And, indeed, in Table 14 it can be seen that this is the case. On the various indices of anxiety, there are only minute and nonsignificant differences between first-born and later-born subjects.

It would perhaps be well to pause briefly in this analytic attempt to understand the factors involved in the relationship of ordinal

TABLE 13

ORDINAL POSITION AND LEVEL OF MANIPULATED ANXIETY
IN HIGH-ANXIETY CONDITIONS

| | a. Hi Anx—Original Experiment | | | b. Hi Irrel | | | |
	N	Anx. 1	No. S's refusing to continue	N	Anx. 1	Anx. 2	No. S's refusing to continue
First-born and only ..	17	3.85	5	18	3.83	3.67	3
Later-born ..	13	3.50	1	25	3.22	2.80	1

| | c. Hi No-Talk* | | | | d. Pooled Hi Anx | | |
	N	Anx.1	Anx.2	No. S's refusing to continue	N	Anx.1	Anx.2	No. S's refusing to continue
First-born and only .	15	4.20	4.67	6	50	3.95	4.12	14
Later-born .	22	3.53	3.64	3	60	3.39	3.19	5
p value of difference between first- and later-born					$<.01$	$<.01$	$<.02$

* Two subjects who answered all of the anxiety questions refused to choose among "Together," "Alone," and "Don't Care." There are consequently two more subjects in this table than in Table 11c.

position to the affiliative reaction to anxiety. The data on anxiety and ordinal positon are rather startling and new. And, though the statistical levels of confidence involved are convincing, this is the sort of serendipitous finding that starts one uneasily searching for confirming data in other studies using other indices of the variables involved. There are, fortunately, relevant data in an experiment conducted by Schachter and Heinzelmann (38). This is a study concerned with the effects of cognitive content on anxiety and time

TABLE 14

ORDINAL POSITION AND LEVEL OF MANIPULATED ANXIETY
IN LOW-ANXIETY CONDITIONS

	a. Lo Anx—Original Experiment			*b. Lo Irrel*			
	N	*Anx. 1*	No. S's refusing to continue	*N*	*Anx. 1*	*Anx. 2*	No. S's refusing to continue
First-born and only..	13	2.23	0	14	2.57	2.36	0
Later-born..	16	2.59	0	27	2.33	2.32	1

	c. Lo No-Talk				*d. Pooled Lo Anx.*			
	N	*Anx.1*	*Anx.2*	No. S's refusing to continue	*N*	*Anx.1*	*Anx.2*	No. S's refusing to continue
First-born and only..	18	2.83	2.56	1	45	2.58	2.47	1
Later-born..	13	2.39	2.31	0	56	2.42	2.31	1
p value of difference between first- and later-born						n.s.	n.s.	n.s.

perception. It is a rather complicated, six-condition experiment, and there is no reason to detail here the experimental procedure involved other than to mention that in this study the subjects, all girls, were actually shocked. Each subject received three series of shocks. Each series consisted of up to twenty-four shocks systematically increasing in intensity in steps of approximately 2 volts. The first shock administered was 2 volts, the current was turned on for three seconds, then turned off briefly, the voltage upped to 4 volts, the current turned on for three seconds again, and so on up to a maximum, if the subject permitted, of 48 volts, at which point the sensation was somewhat unpleasant and painful. There were three series of such shocks, and in each series the subject was asked to tell the experimenter when she first felt the current, when it became painful, and when it became unbearable and she wanted the experimenter to stop. As they relate to ordinal position, the results of the three series are similar, and Table 15 presents the results of one such series.

TABLE 15

ORDINAL POSITION AND TOLERANCE OF PAIN

	No. S's at maximum shock	*No. S's below maximum shock*
First-born and only.......	16	43
Later-born	28	28
	$X^2 = 6.37$	$p < .02$

The column in Table 15 labeled "Maximum Shock" tallies the number of subjects who went up to the full 48 volts without asking the experimenter to stop. The column labeled "Below Maximum Shock" records the number of subjects who requested the experimenter to stop before the shock intensity reached this 48-volt maximum. It is clear from this table that first-born and only children are considerably less willing or able to withstand pain than are later-born children. Fifty percent of all later-born subjects take maximum shock and only 27 percent of first-born and only subjects do so.

There is, then, consistency among all of these experimental results. When exposed to an anxiety-producing situation, first-borns become more anxious and fearful than later-borns.* When directly

---

* One experiment to be presented fully in Chapter 8 yields results which are partially supportive of, partially contradictory to this relationship. On measures of anxiety similar to those used in these anxiety-affiliation experiments, first-born subjects are again more frightened than later-born subjects. On a very different measure of anxiety, there are no differences between the two groups of subjects. Interpretation of these findings demands a fairly detailed knowledge of the experiment, and we shall postpone discussion to Chapter 8.

exposed to the source of anxiety, first-borns do not withstand pain nearly as well as later-borns. All of this, then, would make it appear that the results in Table 11 can be explained by differential anxiety; that is, in high-anxiety conditions first-borns chose "Together" more often than later-borns because they were more anxious.

It is still possible, however, that the second factor is operating; that is, that the link between anxiety and affiliation is stronger for first-borns than for later-borns. Despite the fact that first-borns, in general, respond to the experimental situation with considerably more anxiety than do later-borns, it may still be the case that when these two groups are matched for degree of anxiety, there will be differences in the affiliative nature of their reactions. And, in order to test for this, it is necessary to compare the choices of "Together," "Alone," and "Don't Care" of equally anxious groups of first- and later-born subjects. This comparison is drawn in Table 16, where the data presented represent the choices of all truly anxious subjects. A truly anxious subject is defined here in precisely the same fashion as in the preceding chapter. Any subject who checked either of the two extreme points on the "Anx 1" scale or who indicated that she did not wish to continue in the experiment is considered a truly anxious subject. It can be seen here that the reason we have consistently used the "Anx 1" scale to distinguish between truly high- and truly low-anxiety subjects is to be able to include subjects from the original experiment in this particular analysis. Again it should be pointed out that the correlation between the two scales of anxiety is +.76 and that for the "Irrel" and "No-Talk" conditions the pattern of the results is almost identical no matter which of these two scales is used to distinguish truly high- and low-anxiety groups of subjects.

Table 16 includes subjects from all six experimental conditions. In the pooled Table 16*d* there is a total of 76 subjects. Of these, 66 are from the three high-anxiety conditions and 10 from the three low-anxiety conditions. The pattern of the results is precisely the same in these two sets of conditions.

It can be seen from Table 16 that when the degree of anxiety

TABLE 16

ORDINAL POSITION AND REACTION TO ANXIETY IN ALL
TRULY ANXIOUS SUBJECTS

	a. Original Experiment No. choosing		*b. Irrel Talk* No. choosing	
	Together	Don't Care and Alone	Together	Don't Care and Alone
First-born and only	9	2	13	2
Later-born	3	6	4	10

	c. No Talk No. choosing		*d. Pooled Data* No. choosing	
	Together	Don't Care and Alone	Together	Don't Care and Alone
First-born and only	10	4	32	8
Later-born	4	9	11	25

$$X^2 = 18.86$$
$$p < .001$$

is held constant, first-born and only subjects overwhelmingly chose "Together" and later-born subjects preponderantly did not. Of all truly anxious first-born subjects, 80 percent chose "Together"; of equally anxious later-born subjects, only 31 percent chose "Together." And this is a difference which is significant at considerably better than the .0001 level of confidence. If, in reeling off these zeroes, we manage to create the impression of stringing pearls on a necklace, we rather hope the reader will be patient and forbearing, for it has been the very number of zeroes after this decimal point that has compelled us to treat these data with complete seriousness.

In summary, then, this series of analyses leads to two main conclusions:

First, when they are anxious, first-born and only children are considerably more likely to want to be together with other people than are later-born children. This is an anxiety-specific reaction, for there are no differences in this respect under non-anxiety producing conditions.

Second, in terms of the demonstrated relationship between anxiety and affiliation, the effects of ordinal position might be attributed either to differential anxiety or to differential strength of the link between anxiety and affiliation. In fact, both factors seem to be operating. In anxiety-producing situations, first-born and only children are more anxious than later-born children; and, with degree of anxiety analytically held constant, first-born and only children are considerably more prone to want to be with people than are later-born children.

Let us return now to consideration of the pattern of findings that prompted this examination of the effects of ordinal position on the variables under consideration. It will be recalled that while the trends in the original experiment were clear-cut there were only slight between-condition differences in the "Irrel" and "No-Talk" conditions, and internal analysis was necessary to bring out the relationship of anxiety to the affiliative tendency. It is evident, by now, that the relationship between anxiety and the affiliative tendency holds for early-born individuals and hardly at all for later-born individuals. Comparison of Tables 11 and 12 makes it clear that in each of the experiments first-born and only subjects in high-anxiety conditions chose "Together" far more often than their counterparts in the low-anxiety conditions, whereas no such trend is evident for later-born subjects. All of this implies, of course, that the sampling distribution of first- and later-born subjects in the several conditions might have a strong effect on between-condition differences. If, for example, a high-anxiety condition had, by chance, an exceptionally large proportion of later-born subjects, there should be relatively little difference between the high- and correspondingly low-anxiety conditions in the proportion of "Together" choices. Examination of the distribution of subjects by ordinal position in Table 11 indicates that something of this sort has occurred in these experiments. In the original experiment, where between-condition differences were large, 56.7 percent of the subjects in the "Hi Anx" condition were first-born and only children. In the "Hi Irrel" condition 41.9 percent, and in the "Hi No-Talk" condition 37.1 percent of the subjects were first-born and only children. It would appear, then, that this particular distribution of subjects is in good part responsible for the small between-condition differences obtained in the "Irrel" and "No-Talk" versions of this experiment. This series of findings does, then, permit considerably more confidence in the conclusions and interpretations reached in Chapter 4, for it is no longer necessary to temper these conclusions with the qualifications inevitably imposed by an internal analysis. Though for the moment these conclusions appear to be limited to first-born and only subjects, it is clear that in each of the experimental conditions there is a positive relationship between anxiety and the affiliative tendency.

In the succeeding chapter, the broader implications of this series of findings on the effects of ordinal position will be examined more closely. For the remainder of this section, however, this particular body of data will be examined for the effects of family size, for differences, if any, between only and first children, and for the effects of absolute ordinal position.

THE EFFECTS OF FAMILY SIZE

Throughout this discussion, it has been implied that these various findings have been a function of ordinal position, and there has been no consideration of the possible artifactual effects of family size. Family size is a possibly confounding variable, for of course the larger the family, the greater the number of later-born children. It is conceivable, then, that these results are due to differences in family size, rather than to differences in ordinal position. If this is the case, it might be expected that if family size is held constant there would be no differences in ordinal position, but if subjects from large and small families are compared there would be major differences along the several dimensions here delineated. This is a particularly important point to pursue, for if this expectation should turn out to be correct it would suggest that rather than search for explanatory variables which one might guess would be related to ordinal position, we should search in the realm of factors such as rural-urban differences, religious differences, socio-economic status, and so on, which are known to be related to family size.

To evaluate the effects of family size, it is necessary only to compare first-born and later-born children in families of various sizes. A first step toward such a comparison is made in Table 17, where the subjects are categorized as coming from small families (two or three children) or large families (four or more children). In addition, for later purposes, this table includes data for one-child families. Table 17 includes all subjects from the three high-anxiety conditions. The figures in this table represent for each category

TABLE 17

EFFECTS OF FAMILY SIZE ON THE PROPORTION OF SUBJECTS CHOOSING
TOGETHER IN HIGH-ANXIETY CONDITIONS (POOLED DATA)

	Family Size					
	1 child		*2-3 children*		*4+ children*	
	N	*% S's choosing Together*	N	*% S's choosing Together*	N	*% S's choosing Together*
First-born and only....	10	70	24	83.3	14	35.7
Later-born ...			33	45.5	27	22.2

the proportion of subjects choosing the "Together" alternative. For both small and large families, first-borns chose "Together" relatively more often than later-borns. However, there are striking differences between small and large families. In large families, both first- and later-borns chose "Together" considerably less often than their counterparts in small families, and the difference between first-and later-born children is considerably smaller in large families than in small families.

In order to understand these differences between small and large families, it will be necessary to repeat the analytic procedures previously employed, for, again, it is possible that these differences are due either to differential anxiety or to differential strength of the link between anxiety and affiliation. Data on anxiety are presented in Table 18, where it is evident that the pattern of the data is essentially the same as in the previous table. There is a consider-

TABLE 18

EFFECTS OF FAMILY SIZE ON ANXIETY IN HIGH-ANXIETY CONDITIONS
(POOLED DATA)

	Family Size							
	1 child			*2–3 children*			*4+ children*	
		% S's re-fusing to con-			% S's re-fusing to con-			% S's re-fusing to con-
	N	Anx 1	tinue	N	Anx 1	tinue	N	Anx 1	tinue
First-born and only...	10	3.95	0	26	4.23	42.3	14	3.43	21.4
Later-born ..				33	3.38	12.1	27	3.29	3.7

able difference in the anxiety level of first-born and later-born subjects from small families and a smaller difference between corresponding groups in large families. Subjects from large families are less frightened than subjects from small families.* All of this, then,

* This difference between subjects from small and large families is probably understandable in terms of rural-urban and socio-economic differences. Though there are no data available on the socio-economic status of these subjects, there is good evidence that subjects from large families are more frequently from rural backgrounds than subjects from small families. The home towns of 43.2 percent of the subjects from large families have populations of 1500 or less while only 12.1 percent of subjects from small families had home towns this small. It is con-

would certainly make it appear that differential anxiety is the explanation for these differences between subjects from small and large families.

If it is correct that anxiety is the responsible variable, it is to be expected that there will be similarity in the pattern of responses of subjects from large and small families when anxiety is held constant and the affiliative responses of the truly anxious subjects in these three experimental conditions are compared. An examination of the data presented in Table 19 indicates that this is indeed the case. For these subjects there are very large differences between

TABLE 19

EFFECTS OF FAMILY SIZE ON THE REACTIONS TO ANXIETY
OF ALL TRULY ANXIOUS SUBJECTS

	Family Size					
	1 child		*2–3 children*		*4+ children*	
	N	*% S's choosing Together*	N	*% S's choosing Together*	N	*% S's choosing Together*
First-born and only	9	77.8	24	83.3	7	71.4
Later-born			21	42.9	15	13.3

ceivable that subjects from rural or relatively poor homes are simply tougher and more impervious to the brand of threat implied in the experimental manipulation. There is evidence, too, that subjects from large families had had more direct experience with electricity than subjects from small families. In the original experiment, after the catharsis period, all of the subjects answered a brief questionnaire asking about their experience with electricity (e.g., repairing electrical gadgets) and inquiring as to whether or not they had ever been shocked. Thirty-three percent of the subjects from large families admitted to some kind of experience and only 12 percent of subjects from small families had any such experience. Ninety-two percent of subjects from large families had at some time been shocked, compared with 70 percent of subjects from small families. Conceivably, familiarity of this sort could greatly diminish the effect of a manipulation whose impact depends upon fear of electricity.

first-borns and later-borns in both small and large families. The proportion of first-borns and later-borns choosing "Together" is not significantly different for small or large families. The single difference sizeable enough to warrant attention is the quite low proportion of later-borns from large families who chose "Together" as compared with later-borns from small families. The explanation for this difference will become clear when the effects of absolute ordinal position are considered.

The gist of this analysis seems clear-cut: the variable determining the affiliative nature of the response to anxiety appears to be ordinal position and not family size. The family-size variable does appear to have an effect on the level of anxiety, but this effect seems understandable in terms of rural-urban and socio-economic differences of subjects from small and large families.

ONLY CHILD VERSUS FIRST CHILD

In terms of popular concern with the problems of the only child and with the effects of sibling rivalry on the oldest child, it may be of some interest to compare the data for first-born and only subjects. Such a comparison will allow evaluation of the effects, if any, that a child's having *younger* siblings has on the several variables with which these studies are concerned. The relevant data are contained in Tables 17, 18, and 19, where one-child families are compared with larger families.

The affiliative nature of the reaction to anxiety is much the same for only children and first children. In Table 17 it can be seen that in the high-anxiety conditions only children chose "Together" just about as frequently as did the first children of small families. And comparing the truly anxious subjects in Table 19, it is clear that there is almost no difference between only children and the first children of either small or large families in the extent to which these groups chose "Together."

On the degree of anxiety or nervousness felt about taking part in the experiment, there is some inconsistency in the data. In Table 18 it can be seen that on the "Anx 1" measure the scores of only children are only slightly and nonsignificantly lower than the scores of first children from small families. There are large differences, however, in the extent to which first-born and only subjects are willing to continue in the experiment. Every subject who was an only child was willing to continue, while some 42 percent of the first-born subjects from small families refused to continue. This difference appears to be due in part at least to a quirk of sampling (a quirk because in scheduling subjects, the experimenter of course had no knowledge of a subject's ordinal position), for 8 of the 10 only children in high-anxiety conditions were in the "Hi Irrel" condition. Of the three high-anxiety conditions, it will be remembered, the manipulation of anxiety was least effective in this condition. This cannot be the entire explanation, however, for 3 of the 10 first children in the "Hi Irrel" condition refused to continue in the experiment as compared with 0 of 8 only children. This last, of course, is the only meaningful comparison that can be made on this point. However, the data available are simply too scanty to allow for any conclusions, and the point must remain at issue.

On the affiliative nature of the response to anxiety, however, there is no ambiguity, and within the limits of the sample sizes available, there is no evidence of a difference in this respect between first and only children.

THE EFFECTS OF EXACT ORDINAL POSITION

In all of the analyses presented so far, the simple dichotomy "first-born vs. later-born" has been employed, and the category "later-born" has included subjects whose ordinal positions ranged from second to seventh in their families of origin. The issue may well be raised, then, as to whether or not these effects are continuous; that is, is the affiliative response to anxiety stronger for second children than for third children, stronger for third children than for fourth children, and so on.

The relevant data are plotted in Figure 1, which includes the affiliative responses of all truly anxious subjects in both high- and low-anxiety conditions. The percentage of subjects choosing the

"Together" alternative is plotted along the ordinate. Ordinal position is noted along the abscissa. The position 4+ includes, of course, all fourth children as well as two fifth and one seventh child. The several curves separate the data for subjects originating from 2, 3, and 4+ child families. The 4+ curve includes the data of nine subjects coming from 5, 6, 7, and 9 child families.

Examination of these curves makes it plain that the affiliative response to anxiety is strongly related to exact ordinal position. For every family size, there is a constant and sizeable decrease in the proportion of subjects choosing "Together" as ordinal position increases. In families with four children, for example, first children chose "Together" more often than did second, second children more often than third, and third more often than fourth. And precisely the same trend holds for all other family sizes. It should be noted, too, that from ordinal position to position there is no overlap in the distribution of the points plotted. For first children the range is from 71.4 percent to 100 percent; for second children the range is from 45.5 percent to 60 percent, and for third children from 16.7 percent to 20 percent. This may be taken as some indication that exact ordinal position is the crucial variable and that there is no interaction between the effects of family size and of ordinal position.

The cumulated frequencies of the data plotted in the curves are recorded in Table 20, where family size is ignored and the distribution of choices of all truly anxious subjects at each ordinal position is recorded. And, of course, these data document once more the relationship discussed above. Eighty percent of first-born and only subjects chose "Together," 50 percent of second-borns chose "Together," 18 percent of third-borns did so, and none of the subjects whose ordinal position is fourth or greater did so. It seems patently clear, then, that whatever the variables that determine these differences between early- and late-born children, they operate in a continuous fashion and their effects are strongest for early-born children and grow progressively weaker the later born the child.

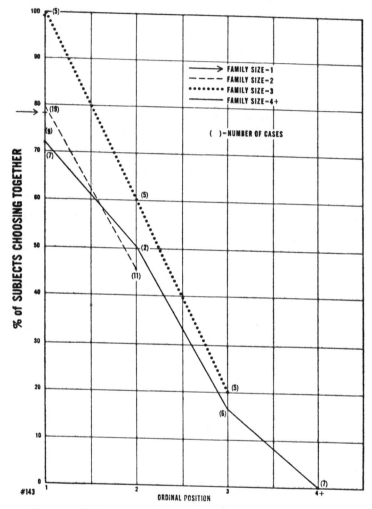

Figure 1. The relationship of ordinal position and family size to the choice of "Together" by "Truly Anxious" subjects.

TABLE 20

EFFECTS OF ORDINAL POSITION ON REACTIONS TO ANXIETY
OF ALL TRULY ANXIOUS SUBJECTS

	No. choosing	
Ordinal Position	*Together*	*Don't Care and Alone*
1 and only	32	8
2	9	9
3	2	9
4+	0	7
	$X^2 = 24.99$	$p < .001$

One additional item should be recorded here. Though we have not discussed the relationship of absolute ordinal position to the level of anxiety, it should be noted that much the same trend holds for this variable. Thus, 28 percent of all first-born and only subjects in high-anxiety conditions refused to continue in the experiment, 11.1 percent of second-borns, 6.3 percent of third-borns, and 5.9 percent of subjects who are fourth- or later-born. And, again, this trend holds for families of all sizes, though, as is to be expected from our earlier discussion of anxiety, differences between adjacent ordinal positions are considerably smaller for large families than for small families.

To summarize the major findings noted in these sub-analyses:

1. Family size has no effect on the affiliative response of anxious subjects.

2. Having *younger* siblings appears to have no effect on subjects' affiliative responses, for there are no differences in this respect between only and first children. There are some indications, however, that only children are somewhat less frightened than first-born children.

3. Absolute ordinal position has a strong relationship to the affiliative response of anxious subjects, for the later the subject's birth position, the less the likelihood that she will choose "Together."

6

Ordinal Position, Anxiety, and Affiliation—II

The results of this analysis of the effects of ordinal position on the affiliative response to anxiety are dramatic and startling, and the question immediately arises: to what extent can these experimental results be generalized for real-life situations? Are the variables mediated by ordinal position so powerful that in real life analogies to this laboratory situation, the same pattern of relationships emerges? Let us begin examination of these questions by considering the finding that later-born subjects when anxious did not particularly wish to be with other people. Whimsically, this may suggest, among other things, an alcoholic, that is, a troubled person who is not strongly inclined to handle his difficulties by social means and seeks to dispose of his problems by drinking. Now if the analogy applies to the demonstrated experimental relationship, it should follow that later-borns will be overrepresented among chronic alcoholics and early-borns underrepresented. And the evidence indicates that this is indeed the case. In his article "The Relationship Between Alcoholism and Birth Rank" (4), David Bakan analyzes the ordinal position of two samples of chronic alcoholic males.* The major body of his data is reproduced in Table 21. Bakan summarizes these data in the following words:

> The statistical hypothesis which will be tested is that for individuals coming from family sizes such as those found in the sample, the probability of any individual being in any birth rank appropriate to that family size is the same. . . . Under the hypothesis, a chi-square value of 1,026.743 would occur by chance for 9 degrees of freedom so very infrequently ($p < .001$) that the hypothesis is definitely rejected. We may therefore conclude that the likelihood of an individual contributing to the

population sampled is related to his birth rank. Examining the directions of deviation from expectation, and the associated chi-square values for each birth rank, it seems that the likelihood for contributing to the sampled population increases as birth rank increases. The population of alcoholics draws disproportionately from the general population as a function of birth rank. It draws most heavily from those who have older siblings, in accordance with the number of older siblings, and draws least heavily from those who are older siblings. (Pp. 434–36.)

It would certainly appear, then, that conforming to expectations stimulated by these experimental studies, later-borns are disproportionately represented among chronic alcoholics. The similarity

TABLE 21*

ORDINAL POSITION AND ALCOHOLISM

Obtained frequencies in sample of alcoholics, theoretical frequencies under hypothesis of no relationship, and chi-square values
(229 only children excluded)

Birth Rank	Obtained Frequency	Theoretical Frequency under Hypothesis	Chi-Square
1	180	344.5	78.549
2	324	344.5	1.220
3	216	222.0	0.162
4	160	143.3	1.946
5	127	95.3	10.544
6	71	54.7	4.857
7	68	33.0	37.121
8	33	17.6	13.475
9	43	7.8	158 851
10	42	2.2	720.018

Total   1,026.743

* Reproduced from D. Bakan, "The Relationship Between Alcoholism and Birth Rank" (4).

between the trend of Bakan's data and the trend reported in Figure 1 and Table 20 should be noted. The later born the subject the less the probability that she would choose "Together" when really anxious. Similarly Bakan concludes, "the likelihood for contributing to the sampled population increases as birth rank increases."

One cautionary note must be injected. The major body of Bakan's data is presented in such form that it is impossible to correct for the possible effects of family size. Though it is exceedingly unlikely (particularly when we examine the extent to which the obtained exceed the theoretical frequencies for the later-birth ranks) that family size could entirely account for differences of this magnitude, general sociological knowledge makes it seem likely that to some extent these differences are exaggerated by the artifactual effects of family size. In this same paper, Bakan presents data for 100 cases of alcoholism in a fashion which does make it possible to separate the effects of birth rank and family size. Though the number of cases is far too small to permit any definitive conclusion, there are indications that ordinal position, independent of family size, is a determining variable of these effects.

ORDINAL POSITION AND PSYCHOTHERAPY

Let us return once again to the basic finding that under conditions of anxiety, first-born and only children overwhelmingly choose to be with other people, whereas later-born children do not. From this indication that the magnitude of the force to seek other people is greater for anxious first-borns than for equally anxious later-borns it could reasonably be assumed that when anxious and in the presence of other people first-borns would be more likely to try to prolong this social relationship than would later-borns. Further, it *might* be assumed that being with others serves as a more effective anxiety-reducing device for first-borns than for later-borns.

Clearly both of these assumptions go far beyond the immediate findings on ordinal position, anxiety, and affiliation. However, in the light of these findings, they may certainly be considered reasonable assumptions and they do suggest testable implications. Consider the nature of psychotherapy, clearly a procedure by which a troubled person seeks out a form of social help rather than attempting to handle his problems by himself. If these findings are capable of generalization and if these additional assumptions are correct, it should be anticipated first that first-borns would be more likely to seek psychotherapeutic help and second that first-borns would remain in psychotherapy for longer periods than later-borns.

Before considering relevant data, one earlier question must be treated. Is there any evidence that early-born individuals are any more anxious or troubled by psychological conditions that would send them to a psychotherapist than are later-born individuals? Though we have been free in our use of the term "anxiety," it should be made clear that the experimental manipulations have involved nothing more than the manipulation of physical fear. Though demonstrably first-born subjects reacted with more fear to a given fear-provoking situation than did later-born subjects, there is absolutely no reason to expect from this finding that first-born individuals might generally be more psychologically disturbed than later-born individuals. And what evidence there is indicates no difference in this respect between early- and later-born individuals. A variety of studies (29, 46, 49, 55), using tests such as the Thurstone neurotic inventory, the Bernreuter Personality Inventory, and Terman's adaptation of the Woodworth-Matthews Personal Data Sheet, have consistently failed to demonstrate any relationship between ordinal position and psychological states of disturbance variously labeled "emotional instability," "neuroticism," and "maladjustment."

To add our own bit to this parade of negative findings, Tables 22*a* and 22*b* present the results of an administration of the Taylor Manifest Anxiety Scale (47) to 298 students in undergraduate psychology classes at the University of Minnesota. These tables allow evaluation of the effects of both ordinal position and family size for males and females separately. The recorded figures represent mean manifest anxiety scores. The greater the score, the greater

TABLE 22

MANIFEST ANXIETY AND ORDINAL POSITION

| | | *a. Females* | | | |
| | | Birth Rank | | | |
		1	2	3	4+
Family Size: No. of children	1	12.58 (12)			
	2	12.34 (23)	11.00 (17)		
	3	11.73 (11)	14.22 (9)	14.50 (6)	
	4+	15.80 (10)	13.13 (8)	12.80 (5)	10.00 (11)

| | | *b. Males* | | | |
| | | Birth Rank | | | |
		1	2	3	4+
Family Size: No. of children	1	13.38 (26)			
	2	11.70 (33)	13.35 (17)		
	3	13.72 (32)	17.50 (10)	13.30 (10)	
	4+	10.65 (17)	10.50 (14)	14.50 (10)	11.18 (17)

the manifest anxiety. The figures in brackets are the number of cases in each cell of the table. Inspection of these tables reveals no indication of any systematic trends, most of the differences may be dismissed as chance fluctuations, and the conclusion may be drawn that there is no relationship between psychological disturbance as measured by this particular index and ordinal position.

Again, on a variety of behavioral indices of disturbance there appears to be no clear-cut relationship with ordinal position. For delinquency, for example, there exists a body of completely contradictory evidence. Sletto (45) finds some indication that early-born children tend more to delinquency than later-born children, whereas Baker, Decker, and Hill (5) find no evidence of such a relationship. Burt (8) reports that only children are overrepresented among delinquent boys and Slawson (44) finds no such relationship. Similarly contradictory evidence exists on the relationship of ordinal position to behavior problems. Where Rosenow and Whyte (34) find that a slightly larger proportion of first-born children than would be expected by chance are brought as problem children to child-guidance clinics, Levy (32) does not find consistent indications of such a relationship in a similar study. Examined en masse, the many studies on ordinal position and various indicators of behavioral disorder present a pattern of negative results and of weak and inconsistent trends.

To the extent that these various results may be credited as indications that psychological disturbance is not related to ordinal position, we may proceed with an examination of the relationship of ordinal position to the acceptance and duration of psychotherapy in the assurance that any relationship revealed is not confounded by differences in the degree of disturbance.

Data on ordinal position and psychotherapy are available from a still unpublished study conducted by Wiener and Stieper (54).* This study is concerned with psychometric prediction of the duration and outcome of outpatient psychotherapy. The subjects of this study were 150 individuals who applied to the outpatient department of the Mental Hygiene Clinic at the Veterans Administration Center at Fort Snelling, Minnesota. These are all white, male veterans with nervous disorders incurred or aggravated in the service. Of these 150 cases, data on ordinal position were available for 132 individuals; the data for these individuals are recorded in Table 23.

Almost all of these people were on some sort of government disability pension, for their nervous disorders were incurred or ag-

---

* We wish to thank Dr. Donald Stieper for his generosity in making these data available and for carrying out the special analyses required to test the points here at issue.

gravated in the service. By law all veterans holding disability pensions are required to report to a Veterans Administration hospital at roughly annual intervals for a check-up examination. Veterans on pension for psychological disturbances report to a neuropsychiatric examiner, who during his interview will as a rule mention the availability of free therapeutic help in the VA. As a matter of policy no deliberate attempt is made to pressure the veteran into accepting therapy.

On the acceptance and duration of psychotherapy the possible indices are clear-cut and derive from a common-sense depiction of the process that a possible patient goes through in deciding whether or not to go into therapy and whether or not to continue in therapy. Initially the individual simply presents himself for a routine examination, where the possibility of getting this kind of psychological help is mentioned. The individual decides whether or not he will go into therapy. Assuming he decides to enter treatment, he may sample a few therapeutic hours and, on the basis of this experience, again make a decision as to whether to go seriously into the process or to drop the whole business. Therapy may go on for an indeterminate length of time, though finally a decision is made to terminate the process.

From the experimental findings and the additional assumptions made, it follows that first-born patients will be more inclined to accept therapy and to prolong the process than will later-born patients. Just what role and weight to assign the therapist in the decision to terminate is, of course, an unsettled question. For this particular group of patients, however, it does appear that the patient is chiefly responsible for the decision to terminate. In a personal communication on the matter, Dr. Stieper has written, "Although we do not have sufficient experimental data at this point, the mass of subjective evidence seems to indicate that the patient is the major determinant of when termination occurs; he quits because he feels he isn't getting anything, or that he has gotten well enough, or something interferes (such as a change of job) to prevent him from continuing." It is anticipated, then, that:

1. First-born individuals will be more inclined to go into therapy than later-borns.

2. First-born patients will be less inclined to drop out of therapy after a token sampling of the process than later-born patients.

3. If, following the initial routine examination, the decision is made to enter psychotherapy, first-born patients will remain in treatment longer than later-borns.

The relevant data are presented in Table 23, where the subjects are divided into three categories: nonaccepters or subjects who, after routine examination, did not go into therapy; token-accepters or subjects who went into therapy but stayed in treatment for three treatments or less—a cutoff point used by Wiener and Stieper to distinguish between those who accept only token therapy and those who enter seriously into the process; accepters or subjects who

TABLE 23

ORDINAL POSITION AND PSYCHOTHERAPY

	Only	First-born	Later-born
Number of cases	10	29	93
Percentage of Nonaccepters	10.0	13.8	17.2
Percentage of Token-Accepters	10.0	10.3	23.7
Percentage of Accepters...........	80.0	75.9	59.1
Mean No. of months in therapy (not including nonaccepters).....	25.56	15.56	10.06

stayed in treatment for more than three interviews. The data do conform to expectations. Of the 93 later-born individuals, 17.2 percent were nonaccepters whereas 12.8 percent of 39 first-born and only individuals were nonaccepters. Some 23.7 percent of later-born cases were token-accepters compared with 10.3 percent of first-born and only cases. All told, then, 40.9 percent of the later-born cases never got seriously involved in treatment compared with the 23.1 percent of first-born and only individuals who never became involved. Putting these data into a 2 × 2 table yields a chi-square which, with one degree of freedom, is significant at the

.05 level of confidence. It does appear that disturbed later-born individuals are more reluctant to accept the form of social help represented by psychotherapy than are disturbed first-born and only individuals.

For those who do go into therapy, whether they are token or full accepters, how long do they remain in treatment? The line labeled "mean number of months in therapy" in Table 23 records the relevant data. First-born and only patients averaged 18.1 months in treatment, and later-born patients averaged 10.1 months, a difference which is significant at considerably beyond the .01 level of confidence. The difference between only patients and first-born patients is not significant. The difference between only children and later-borns is significant at the .001 level, and between first-born and later-born at the .08 level of confidence. It should be noted that this pattern of differences maintains itself even if one considers only the seriously involved, full accepters. For this group (all of whom have been in therapy for more than three treatments) first-born and only patients average 20.5 months in treatment as compared with 13.0 months for later-born patients, a difference significant at approximately the .03 level of confidence.

Other studies (25) of factors affecting the duration of therapy have indicated that social class is a determinant, with middle-class patients remaining in therapy for longer periods than lower-class patients. Since it is known that social class is related to family size, it is clear that once more it will be necessary to examine the effects of family size. Table 24 presents the necessary breakdown of the data. The figures in this table represent the mean duration of therapy in months for all patients (both token and full accepters) who actually entered therapy. Comparisons are presented only for family sizes up to six children. There are no first-born patients from families any larger than six. Examination of this table makes it clear that ordinal position is the responsible variable and that family size exercises no artifactual effect. For each family size the duration of psychotherapy is considerably greater for first-born patients than for later-born patients.

TABLE 24

DURATION OF PSYCHOTHERAPY IN MONTHS, AS RELATED
TO ORDINAL POSITION AND FAMILY SIZE

	Family Size (No. children)				
	2	3	4	5	6
First-born: Months in therapy	12.1	26.5	23.0	13.0	13.0
Number of cases	(14)	(2)	(5)	(3)	(1)
Later-born: Months in therapy	3.67	12.4	10.4	8.9	6.0
Number of cases............	(6)	(13)	(11)	(13)	(7)

One final item of information is probably worth recording. Once the individual has decided either not to enter therapy at all or, after a course of treatment, to terminate the process, he may at any time decide to reapply to the VA for treatment. The several considerations that have led to this analysis of ordinal position and responsiveness to psychotherapy would again suggest that first-born and only patients would be more likely to make such reapplication than would later-born patients. And, again, the data bear out this expectation, for 35.9 percent of all first-born and only cases did reapply, as compared with the 20.4 percent of later-born cases—a difference significant by chi-square test at approximately the .07 level of confidence.

To summarize, evidence has been presented indicating that disturbed first-born individuals do seek out and accept the form of social help represented by psychotherapy. If the individual enters treatment, first-born and only patients remain in treatment for considerably longer periods than do later-born patients. These findings should be compared with those on alcoholism, for the two sets of data complement one another neatly. In both cases we are presumably dealing with anxious, troubled, disturbed people. Alcoholism represents an asocial means of coping with disturbance; psychotherapy a social means of handling anxiety. Later-born individuals are relatively more prone to alcoholism, early-born individuals are more susceptible to psychotherapy—a pair of facts which duplicate the basic experimental findings on the effects of ordinal position on the affiliative reaction to anxiety.

One final point can now be made. The interpretation of both the alcoholism and psychotherapy data rests, in part, on the assumption that there is no systematic relationship between ordinal position and psychological disturbance or disorder. Despite the array of evidence mustered to support this assumption, the reader may feel that this point is yet to be proved and that a more sensitive test might indeed demonstrate such a relationship. However, it should be kept in mind that any attempt to explain these data in terms of a relationship between ordinal position and degree of disturbance is virtually forced to predict the same relationship between ordinal position and both alcoholism and susceptibility to psychotherapy (for if both alcoholism and entering therapy are to be interpreted *simply* as reactions to disturbance, they must vary in the same fashion with ordinal position), whereas the data indicate nothing of the kind.

ORDINAL POSITION AND FIGHTER PILOT EFFECTIVENESS

So far, we have examined real-life analogies to the experimentally demonstrated relationship of birth rank to the affiliative reaction to anxiety. But what about anxiety itself? In the experiments, first-born subjects when faced with a standard anxiety-provoking situation responded with considerably more fright and anxiety than later-born subjects. Does this result have any explanatory power outside of the immediate experimental situation?

Let us consider first the relationship between anxiety or fright and performance. It is fairly well accepted that there is a nonmonotonic relationship between these variables, that is, performance improves with small amounts of anxiety and deteriorates with excessive anxiety. It should be anticipated, then, that under really frightening conditions first-born individuals will be less effective than later-born individuals. Combat would seem the ideal locus for testing this expectation; if this line of reasoning is correct, later-born soldiers should make better fighters than early-born soldiers.

The only data available for testing these propositions derives from a study of fighter pilot effectiveness conducted by Paul Torrance* (50). In a way, the situation of the fighter pilot is almost ideal for purposes of this test: first, there is a clear, unambiguous criterion of fighter pilot effectiveness—the number of enemy planes downed; second, the fighter pilot fights alone and his performance is relatively uncontaminated by the multitude of variables affecting performance in group combat. This isolation of the fighter pilot does, however, raise one new question. When the individual faces an anxiety-provoking situation alone, does ordinal position have a differential effect on anxiety? No data have yet been presented on the question, but in terms of what is already known about the effects of ordinal position on the arousal of affiliative needs under anxiety, it is conceivable that being alone in such a situation magnifies the fears of the first-born far more than the fears of the later-born individual. If this is correct, it would imply that the anxiety differential between first and later-born individuals is even greater in solitary combat than in group combat and, again, it should be anticipated that the later-born will be more effective fighter pilots than the early-born individuals.

The purpose and procedure of Torrance's study are best explained in his own words:

> The major purpose of the larger study was to discover why pilots with backgrounds comparable with those of the more successful pilots were not themselves equally successful in combat with the MIG's over Korea. The 38 Air Force aces (pilots with 5 or more MIG-15 kills) accounted for 38.2 percent of the total claims, although they represented less than 5 percent of the pilots completing fighter interceptor tours in Korea. Furthermore, 53.5 percent made no kills at all. . . .
> The subjects of the study are 31 of the 38 aces in air-to-air combat over Korea. Of the seven aces not studied, one was killed in action, one is reported to be held in Manchuria, one was

* We are grateful to Dr. Torrance for making his data available to us in a form which permitted analysis of the effects of ordinal position.

killed in an accident after returning to the States, and the other four were unavailable because of release from the Air Force or the like. Their ages ranged from 24 to 39 years and averaged about 30. Six of those studied are colonels; 3, lieutenant colonels; 6, majors; 13, captains; and 3, first lieutenants. Similar studies were also made of pilots with one to four kills and pilots with no kills, matched for rank, age, and World War II combat experience.

There are, then, three matched groups which we will call aces (5 or more kills), near-aces (1 to 4 kills), and non-aces (0 kills). The distribution of these categories as they relate to ordinal position is presented in Table 25, where it will be noticed that the data conform to expectations. Some 67.7 percent of the aces, 54.6 percent of the near-aces and 41.0 percent of the non-aces are later-

TABLE 25

ORDINAL POSITION AND FIGHTER PILOT EFFECTIVENESS

	Ace (5+ *kills*)	*Near-Ace* (1–4 *kills*)	*Non-Ace* (0 *kills*)
First-born and only	10	15	23
Later	21	18	16
Overall $X^2 = 5.12$		Aces vs. Non-Aces	$X^2 = 4.95$
$d.f. = 2$			$d.f. = 1$
$p = .08$			$p = .03$

borns. It does appear that later-born flyers are more effective fighter pilots. The overall differences in this table are significant at the .08 level of confidence. Comparing the two extreme groups (aces vs. non-aces) yields a chi-square of 4.95, significant with one degree of freedom at the .03 level of confidence.

The experimental result which stimulated this particular analysis was the finding that ordinal position affected the degree of anxiety or fear. Since it is known, from the analyses in Chapter 5 (see particularly Table 18), that family size also affects the magnitude of anxiety, it is obvious that the effects of family size must again be evaluated before any unequivocal conclusions can be drawn. Fortunately, the data are available to permit such an evaluation and they are presented in Table 26, where the cases in each of the three groups are distributed according to ordinal position and family size. Ignoring, momentarily, the data on only children, examination of the sub-table for aces reveals that for each

TABLE 26

EFFECTS OF ORDINAL POSITION AND FAMILY SIZE
ON FIGHTER PILOT EFFECTIVENESS

a. Aces					*b. Near-Aces*			
Family Size (No. children)					Family Size (No. children)			
Ordinal Position	1	2	3	4+	Ordinal Position	1	2	3	4+
1	6	3	0	1	1	3	9	2	1
2		6	4	1	2		4	1	4
3			2	4	3			3	4
4+				4	4+				2

c. Non-Aces			
Family Size (No. children)			
Ordinal Position	1	2	3	4+
1	7	7	6	3
2		2	5	1
3			4	2
4+				2

family size the number of first-borns who are aces is below chance expectancy. Chance expectancies are simply computed by dividing the total number of cases falling in families of a given size by family size; e.g., there are 6 aces originating from 3-child families, if chance alone were operating these 6 cases should be equally distributed among the three ordinal positions with 2 cases at each position. For all of the sub-tables, the figure 5 may be used as a convenient and close approximation to the average number of children in families in the combined category used for families with 4 or more children. For this group of aces, then, family size does not appear to be a confounding variable; for all family sizes there are fewer first-borns than would be expected by chance. The data in the sub-table for non-aces reveal quite the opposite trend. For all family sizes, first-borns occur with greater than chance frequency. There are good indications, then, that the effects noted are a function of ordinal position independent of family size.

The data on only children are of special interest, for they do seem to deviate somewhat from the pattern for first-born flyers. Six of the 10 first-born aces are only children, and these 6 constitute 37.5 percent of the total number of only children in these three groups of pilots. Should this be considered contrary to expectations? Perhaps, but the reader will recall from the discussion of differences between only and first-born subjects in the preceding chapter that there are indications that only children are less fearful than first-born children. In the high-anxiety conditions of the experiments 35 percent of all first-born subjects wanted to drop out of the experiment, while none of the only subjects wanted to drop out. In terms of the differential anxiety explanation of the relationship between fighter pilot effectiveness and ordinal position, these two sets of data can be considered consistent.

If this differential anxiety interpretation is an appropriate explanation of these data on fighter pilots, it should be anticipated that there will be further consistencies with the experimental data. Virtually the sole remaining item for which there are sufficient data to allow meaningful comparison is the effect of family size. It will be recalled (Table 18) that in the experiments subjects from small families were more frightened than subjects from large families. Consistency demands, then, that there be proportionately fewer pilots from small families among the aces than among non-aces. The reverse trend might be expected to obtain for pilots from large families. And the data do tend to conform to these expectations.

Pilots from small families (2–3 children) compose 48.4 percent of the group of aces, 57.6 percent of near-aces, and 61.5 percent of non-aces. Pilots from large families (4+ children) make up 32.3 percent of the aces, 33.3 percent of near-aces, and 20.5 percent of non-aces.

It would be intriguing to compare these data with similar data on bomber pilots. Since the bomber pilot is a member of a crew, such a comparison might permit evaluation of the effect that being a member of a group has on the relationship of ordinal position to pilot effectiveness. If being a member of a group has little or no effect on anxiety level, precisely the same relationships should be expected for bomber pilots as for fighter pilots. If, as earlier speculation suggested, being a member of a group has differential effects on the anxiety levels of first- and later-born individuals, the relationship between ordinal position and pilot effectiveness should be considerably weaker for bomber pilots than for fighter pilots. In any case, the matter must remain unresolved, for discussion with those who have worked extensively on the criterion problem of bomber pilot effectiveness indicates that the highly interdependent nature of bomber crew action has so far made it impossible to hit upon any satisfactory criterion of bomber pilot effectiveness in combat conditions.

To recapitulate, in an attempt to evaluate the extent to which the experimental findings are generalizable, we have searched for real-life situations which, in some fashion, might be considered analogues of the experimental set-up. Independently collected data on alcoholism, psychotherapy, and fighter-pilot effectiveness have been examined for the effects of ordinal position and have at times indicated a remarkable similarity to experimental results. In keeping with the interpretations of experimental results these findings have been interpreted in terms of an interaction among ordinal position, anxiety, and the affiliative tendency. Is an alternative interpretation of any specific finding still possible? Of course, but the marked internal consistency of these several sets of data is, in a way, strong support for the over-all interpretation.

If, at any point, the reader has detected a note of astonishment in this recital of the facts of ordinal position, he has been correct, for we have been rather startled by the magnitude and strength of the experimental differences and truly astonished by the apparent generalizability of these serendipitous findings of laboratory experiments conducted on college girls to male alcoholics, World War II veterans in psychotherapy, and jet pilots in the Korean War. How much farther is it possible to push this ordinal position variable? Apparently not much beyond the confines of the relationship of ordinal position to anxiety and the affiliative tendency, for an abundant research literature has failed to reveal very many consistent relationships with ordinal position. Murphy, Murphy, and Newcomb (33) review some fifty studies conducted up to 1937 on the influence of birth order upon a great variety of individual characteristics (almost all unrelated to present concerns) such as emotional stability, political attitudes, happiness, intelligence, school performance, and a multitude of personality traits. For the most part, these and later studies have been inconclusive and contradictory. Our own single attempt to go beyond the immediate variables and relationships revealed in the experimental studies involved a questionnaire study of sociability. Some three hundred college students responded to a variety of questions on their frequency of dating and of attending parties, on the number of close friends they had, on the number of organizations to which they belonged, and so on. Without an excess of statistical strain, the only one of this mélange of indices of social behavior that revealed any consistent relationship with ordinal position was the number of organizations to which the individual belonged (the earlier the birth rank, the greater the number of organizations). Whether to consider these findings as consistent or inconsistent with the general theme of this chapter is an open question, for interpretation rests on, among other things, decisions as to which of the various possible indices to coordinate with "pure" social drive and which to consider contaminated by the interaction of social drive and the responsiveness of other people.* In any case, the assumptions involved in any interpretation are so arbitrary that it seems best to dismiss these findings as one more instance of confounded, inconclusive research on ordinal position. Though in following sections of this chapter an attempt will be made to broaden the area of behaviors related to ordinal position, it would appear so far that the class of behaviors affected by birth rank is tightly contained within the relationship of anxiety to the affiliative tendency.

And now for the crucial question: how to account for these findings? Certainly ordinal position, in and of itself, is an unsatisfactory, cataloging sort of notion. It has no properties, it has no meaning. It must, however, mediate processes and properties which can account for these findings, and the remainder of this chapter will be concerned with a preliminary stab at identifying these mediated variables. Whatever variables ultimately prove to be mediated by birth rank, it is obvious that their effects must be a result of differences in child-rearing practices as related to ordinal position and of the different consequences of having older or younger siblings around.

Virtually everyone would agree that the first birth is an event of profound psychological and philosophical importance for the parents and that later births are events of considerably less moment. Common sense would suggest that the relative importance of the events plus the experience of the parents would have sweeping general implications for parental feelings about and behavior toward each of their children. One can plausibly expect that with a first child, parents who are still inexperienced and insecure will respond to more signals from the child and respond more quickly than they might with later children. Their insecurity may lead them to overprotect the first child. Their inexperience may force a trial-and-error procedure on them and their behavior with a first

---

* Relevant to this point, there is some reason to expect from a study conducted by Finneran (21) that first-born or only children are less popular than later-born children.

child may be more inconsistent than with later children. With later children one would certainly expect the parents to be more relaxed about the whole business as well as to have considerably less time for paying attention. It is possible, of course, to go on endlessly this way, pointing out plausible reasons for expecting differences in parental behavior as related to ordinal position— but is it true, are there really such differences? Sears, Maccoby, and Levin (42), in their extensive study of patterns of child rearing, have treated this problem, and Table 27 summarizes some of the differences they found on variables that would seem to reflect basic parental attitudes. These data are for the parents of 3- and 4-child families. The trends are precisely the same for 2-child families.

It should be noted first that parents' delight at the prospect of having a child decreases directly with the number of children they already have. The later born the child, the less welcome he seems

TABLE 27

COMPARISON OF CHILD TRAINING OF OLDEST, MIDDLE, AND YOUNGEST
CHIDREN IN THREE- AND FOUR-CHILD FAMILIES

[Adapted from Table D:25 in Sears, Maccoby, and Levin,
Patterns of Child Rearing (42)]

Scales	Oldest	Middle	Youngest	p*
Percentage rated high on:				
Mother delighted when pregnant	58	40	10	< .01
Father delighted when mother pregnant	55	49	15	< .01
Percentage breast-fed	55	43	26	< .05
Median duration of breast feeding for those breast-fed (in months)	4.0	2.1	1.7	n.s.**

* These *p* values are based on· X^2 analysis of the proportions, as given, for the three groups.

** Significant near, but not at, the $p = .05$ level by *F*-test between the three distributions.

to be. Differences in maternal attitude would certainly seem to be reflected in the data on breast-feeding. The later the child, the less the probability that he will be breast-fed and, if breast-fed, the shorter the period of such feeding. These data would certainly seem to indicate rapidly decreasing ardor and interest as the number of children increases, factors which it seems to us would inevitably be communicated to the child. On numerous other specific items of parental behavior there do seem to be strong relationships with ordinal position, but these relationships are frequently so complicated by family size that it is virtually impossible to interpret these differences without further information. The following tendencies should, however, be noted. There seems to be an inconsistency in the training of first-born children that does not characterize the training of later-born children. Parental behavior to first-born children seems to be characterized by considerable permissiveness (to make noise, to show aggression toward younger siblings and neighborhood children, etc.) and at the same time by considerable discipline (restrictions on physical mobility and in large families, at least, frequent physical punishment). For later-born children, the pattern seems more consistent, less permissiveness and less discipline.

In addition to being attributable to differences in parental behavior, these effects of ordinal position may be a consequence of having older or younger siblings. The enormous literature on sibling rivalry is by now so well known that it is pointless to go into any detail on the subject, but the gist of this line of thought may be quickly summarized—the younger child threatens the "throne" of the older child and the older child is a perfect beast to the younger one. If it is assumed that his parents do try to reassure and make up to the first-born child for his displacement and that the first-born child, by the endowment of his years, is constantly punishing his younger sibling for simply being alive, it might be concluded that in the long run the older child represents more of a threat and source of anxiety to the younger one than the younger does to the older child.

For present purposes the effects of the differing psychological environments existing for early- and later-born children may be summarized in two notions—the relative overprotection of first-born children (through which ultimately it may prove possible to explain the differential fear reactions of first- and later-born individuals) and the development of greater dependence in first-born than in later-born children. By dependence we refer to the extent to which the individual uses or relies on other persons as sources of approval, support, help, and reference. Such factors as the inferred differences in amount of parental attention, the existence of an anxiety-provoking person in the later-born child's environment, differential parental protectiveness, and so on lead to this expectation of differential dependence. Of the multitude of variables involved we have simply no idea as to which to hold causally responsible, but Sears et al. (43) and Whiting and Child (53) have suggested an intriguing hypothesis. The development of dependency needs, they suggest, is contingent on two factors—generous amounts of attention and love lavished on the infant and frustration of infantile dependency needs. This hypothesis ties in neatly with the trends noted earlier in the Sears, Maccoby, and Levin study for parental behavior to be more inconsistent and extreme with first-born than with later-born children and does, therefore, lead to the expectation of greater dependence in first-born than in later-born individuals.

This notion of differential dependence or reliance on other people fits our various findings neatly. When they are anxious, first-born subjects want to be with other people and later-born subjects do not. When they are disturbed, first-born individuals seek the social help of psychotherapy more than later-born individuals. This neat fit, however, is scarcely surprising, for these findings generated the search for some sort of explanatory concept that might, with at least some plausibility, be derived from different child-rearing practices. Needless to say, the available data are simply too scanty to allow any considerable confidence in this rough attempt to relate dependence to ordinal position via parental be-

havior; judgment as to whether the notion of differential dependence does anything more than redescribe these findings depends
on whether or not evidence, independent of these specific studies,
supports this identification of dependence as a major variable mediated by ordinal position and whether or not the notion of dependence generates any new predictions about the effects of ordinal
position.

Happily, relevant data are available. Ann Haeberle (27), in the
context of a larger study on dependence and aggression, has analyzed the relationship of dependence to ordinal position.* Her
subjects were three- to six-year-old children attending the therapeutic nursery school of the Child Development Center in New
York City. In general, these were mildly disturbed children, none
of whom was diagnosed as severely psychotic, mentally retarded,
or suffering from organic defects. For each group of nursery school
children (ten to twelve children in a group) there were two teachers who, four times a year, rated each of the children on a variety
of scales designed by Beller (7) to measure overt dependency behavior. Five components of dependency behavior were rated—the
frequency of seeking help, proximity, contact, attention, and recognition from adults in the nursery situation. The summated ratings
provide a dependency score for each child. These scores seem
stable over the course of a year, for statistical test reveals no significant variation in the scores each child received during the four
rating periods.

The relationship of these dependency scores to ordinal position
is presented in Table 28. In making up this table, the average of
the four ratings was used as the dependency score for each child.
With only one exception, all of the children with siblings come
from 2- or 3-child families, with by far the majority originating
in 2-child families. The number of cases is simply too small to
permit any meaningful analysis of the effects of family size but

* We wish to thank Dr. Haeberle for making these unpublished
data available to us. The project from which these data are derived is
under the direction of Dr. E. Kuno Beller.

there is no indication that these trends are in any way a function of family size.

TABLE 28

DEPENDENCY ON ADULTS AND ORDINAL POSITION

	Boys			Girls		
	Only	First Born	Later Born	Only	First Born	Later Born
N	5	7	14	8	14	15
Mean dependency	24.68	19.24	16.16	23.48	21.29	20.31
p^*		$05 > p > .02$			n.s.	

	Boys and Girls		
	Only	First Born	Later Born
N	13	21	29
Mean dependency	23.94	20.61	18.30
p^*		$.01 > p > .001$	

* These p values are based on t tests of the differences between means of only and first-born children vs. later-born children.

The trends are clear. For both boys and girls, only children have higher dependency scores than first-born children and first-born children have higher scores than later-born children. The differences between first-born and only children as against later-born children are significant for the combined groups and for boys alone but not for girls alone. Possibly the fact that the nursery school teachers were women and, more importantly, that the expected and desired pattern of behavior for little girls (being affectionate, cuddly, warm, unaggressive, etc.) overlaps with what is considered dependency behavior on the specific scales used in making these ratings can explain the fact that in these data the relationship between dependence and ordinal position is weaker for girls than for boys. If this is correct, it should be expected that in general the dependency scores of girls should be higher than those of boys. This is the case, the mean score of all girls being 21.37 and of all boys 18.63.

The data presented in Table 28 are for dependency on adults. These same children were rated by their teachers for dependency on other children. Precisely the same five scales were used in making these judgments. The two sets of dependency scores correlate highly, and much the same relationships hold for ordinal position and dependency on other children as for ordinal position and dependency on adults. However, the two sets of ratings were made at precisely the same time (first for adults, immediately after for other children), and since it seems likely that a "halo effect" has confounded these results, no conclusions will be drawn.

For this group of mildly disturbed young children, then, it does appear that behaviors that can reasonably be coordinated with the notion of dependence are systematically related to ordinal position. Does this relationship maintain for more normal populations and with other measures of dependence? Sears (41), in a discussion of ordinal position as a psychological variable, presents previously unpublished material from several studies. In one of these studies, Dean (10) investigated the personality characteristics of children from 20 two-child families by having the mother of each pair of children make paired comparisons of her own children on a large number of personality related items. Differences in ordinal position were found on a number of items, and, consistent with results discussed so far, first-born children were judged by their mothers to be more dependent than their siblings. Further support for this relationship comes from studies by Gewirtz (24) and Beller (6) in which 42 three- and four-year-old children in the University of Iowa preschool were observed under standardized conditions for four hours each over a four-month period and were rated by their teachers on various types of dependency. The observations involved, among other things, frequency counts of various types of nurturant and dependent behavior. The rating scales used were precisely the same as those employed in the study from which Table 28 is derived—ratings of the frequency of seeking help, proximity, contact, attention, and recognition from adults in the nursery school. Again first-born and only children appear to be somewhat more dependent than later children. The differences are small but consistent over a variety of scales and observation schedules. On the basis of this body of evidence, Sears concludes that ordinal position is related to dependency.

In a variety of studies, then, using several distinct measures of dependence, the same relationship obtains—dependency is greater for early-born than for later-born children. It may therefore be that these various data on anxiety and affiliation represent just one manifestation of the relationship between ordinal position and dependence (and certainly an extreme one, for it is reasonable to expect that dependent behavior will be most strongly manifested under conditions of disturbance and emergency). If this is correct, it should be expected that, in general, behaviors which are related to or derived from dependency will be related to ordinal position. In terms of a conception of dependence as the extent to which other people are used as sources of support and reference, it could reasonably be expected that there will be a relationship between dependency and influencibility. Early-born individuals should, then, be more influencible than later-born individuals.

Relevant evidence is available as a by-product of a study of social influence conducted by Danuta Ehrlich (13). In the beginning stage of this experiment, subjects (all male college students) who were assembled in groups of five to seven people were each presented with a write-up of a case study which they were asked to read once. They were then each given a slip of paper listing seven scaled alternative outcomes of this case and asked to indicate privately which of the alternatives they considered to be the most likely outcome. The experimenter collected these slips, pretended to tabulate them, and then on the pretext that it might be interesting for each subject to know how other members of the group felt about this case, the experimenter distributed to each subject a slip of paper on which was tallied the alternatives selected by all of the group members. This "census" had been deliberately prepared to give each subject the impression that he was a deviate. No matter which alternative the subject had originally chosen, the census indicated that he stood alone at this point and that all of the other subjects were massed together, two or three scale points away from the subject. The subjects were then asked to reread the case, think about it further, and on the same scale indicate their final decision as to which was the most likely outcome. Influencibility, then, is measured by the shift in opinion from the first to the second rating.

There were two experimental conditions differing only in that in one condition the subjects believed that their second rating would be completely private and in the other condition that their second rating would become public knowledge. There are interesting differences between the data of these two conditions but they are beyond the scope of our immediate concern and for the analysis of the effects of ordinal position the data of the two conditions are pooled.

The relevant data are presented in Table 29. Any subject who on his second rating came closer to the fictitious group norm is considered a "conformer." A subject who on second rating did not change his original opinion or changed it in a direction away from the group norm is considered a nonconformer. The data do indicate that first-born and only subjects tend to conform more often than later-born subjects. Some 59.3 percent of all first-borns were conformers and 42.5 percent of all later-borns were conformers. Parenthetically it should be noted that though the direction of the

TABLE 29

INFLUENCIBILITY AND ORDINAL POSITION

	No. of Conformers	*No. of Nonconformers*
First-born and only.....	32	22
Later-born	34	46

$$X^2 = 3.62$$
$$p = .06$$

relationship is the same in the two conditions, the effect of ordinal position on influencibility is considerably greater in the private than in the public condition.

All in all, the rudiments of a supporting case can be made for the suggestion that dependence is one of the crucial variables to be mediated by ordinal position. Independent measures of dependence show systematic relationships with ordinal position. Influencibility, which can be plausibly linked to dependence, seems to be related to ordinal position. If this suggestion is correct, other behaviors which are linked to dependency should eventually prove to be systematically related to ordinal position.

So much data and such a diversity of studies have been reported here that it would perhaps be well to summarize the argument of the last two chapters. In a series of experiments concerned with the relationship of anxiety to the affiliative tendency, early-born subjects proved to be more anxious and frightened when faced with a standard anxiety-provoking situation than later-born subjects. When presented with the choice, anxious early-born subjects chose to be together with other subjects whereas equally anxious later-born subjects did not do so. In an attempt to test the generalizability of these findings, real-life analogues of the experimental situation were sought in the expectation that troubled and anxious first-born individuals would tend to seek out social means of handling their anxieties while later-born individuals would be more prone to seek out nonsocial means. Heavy drinking may be considered a nonsocial means of coping with anxiety and later-born individuals prove to be heavily overrepresented among chronic alcoholics. First-born and only individuals are far more susceptible than later-born individuals to the lures of psychotherapy, a social mode of handling anxiety. The question of whether the experimental finding of differential fear as related to ordinal position can be generalized is tested in combat data, and later-born flyers prove to be more effective fighter pilots than first-born flyers.

An attempt is made to formulate these findings in terms of a relationship between ordinal position and dependence. It is assumed that dependent behavior will be most strongly manifested in conditions of disturbance and anxiety but that there should be other nonanxiety related indications of such a relationship. Independent measures of dependence prove to be systematically related to ordinal position, with first-born individuals consistently more dependent than later-born individuals. Influencibility, which is assumed to be in part a function of dependence, is demonstrated to be related to ordinal position. It is anticipated that other dependency-linked behaviors will eventually prove to be related to ordinal position.

7

*H*unger and *A*ffiliation

The initial experiment described resulted in the formulation "anxiety leads to the arousal of affiliative tendencies." The last four chapters have described studies concerned with two elements of this formulation: an attempt to analyze experimentally the nature of the "affiliative tendency" under conditions of anxiety; and an examination of the consequences of the simple assumption that the "leads to" element of the formulation has its genesis in the long past relationships of the individual. One element of the relationship remains to be explored—anxiety. What precisely is meant by anxiety and what are the limits of the relationship? What order of phenomena leads to the arousal of affiliative tendencies? Though we have freely used the term "anxiety," it is quite clear that the experimental studies have involved only the manipulation of physical fear. Would the same relationships hold for such brands of anxiety as stage fright, test anxiety, job insecurity, and so on? More importantly, what is the conceptual status of the anxiety variable? Should it be considered as an emotional state or as a drive state? Such questions are of course basic to a true understanding of this relationship, for they point directly to the fundamental theoretical problem—for what class of psychological phenomena does this relationship with the affiliative tendency hold?

Consideration of these matters led originally to speculation which at this point seems to us naïve, deceptively oversimplified, and somewhat misleading. Reluctantly, however, it must be admitted that if the reader is to understand precisely why the experiment about to be described was ever undertaken, this original line of argument must be reproduced. Simply put, the banal assumption that the social nature of an individual's reaction to anxiety will be determined by the extent to which people have served as anxiety reducers in the past did lead to a somewhat startling series of findings on the effects of ordinal position. The fruitfulness of this simple assumption led immediately to the notion that anxiety may be only one of a class of drives. Certainly if the child is hungry a person feeds it; if the child is thirsty a person gives it something to drink. In short, for a particular set of drives, people serve as drive reducers for one another, and it might just be that for such drives the affiliative impulse increases directly with drive state. The test of this suggestion required only the manipulation of drive state and a measure of the consequent magnitude of the affiliative tendency.

EXPERIMENTAL PROCEDURE

Since it is comparatively simple to handle experimentally, the hunger drive was manipulated. There were three experimental conditions—high, medium, and low hunger. High hunger entailed a period of approximately 20 hours of food deprivation, medium hunger approximately 6 hours, and low hunger 0 hours of food deprivation.

The subjects were all male undergraduates, students in psychology and social science classes at the University of Minnesota, who had volunteered in their classes to take part in some undescribed "psychological experiment." The evening before the day of an experimental session, volunteers were telephoned and informed that an experiment on the effects of food deprivation on the sensations was to take place on the following afternoon. If they agreed to serve as subjects, which almost everyone did, those people who had been randomly pre-assigned to the high- and low-hunger conditions were asked to go without breakfast and lunch on the following day. Those subjects who were assigned to the medium-hunger condition were asked to eat their normal breakfast at their regular breakfast hour but to do without lunch. To make the experiment somewhat more palatable, all subjects were told that they could drink tea or coffee but no milk. Fairly intensive but gentle questioning after the experiment indicates that all of the subjects abided exactly by these instructions to do without food.

All subjects were asked to come to an experimental room at 2:00 o'clock on the afternoon following this phone call. Each subject in a particular experimental group was asked to come to a different room. When a subject who had been assigned to the low-hunger condition arrived at his room, he was presented with an appetizing array of cold meats, cheese, bread, cookies, fruit, and coffee, and told:

> As we told you over the phone, this is an experiment concerned with the effects of *particular* kinds of food deprivation and it is necessary for the sake of the experiment that all subjects eat the same kinds of things at precisely the same time interval before the experiment. It is important for the experiment that you eat as much of this food as you like until you are completely satisfied and no longer hungry. Okay?

The experimenter then continued:

> While you are eating we would like you to do one more thing for us. In order to evaluate your reactions in the experiment, we must have information concerning the kinds of food you eat and how often you eat them. I have here a cookbook with a large number of recipes. I would like you to go through the pages listed on this sheet and, following the instructions on the sheet, list those dishes you have eaten and how frequently you have eaten them.

When subjects assigned to high- and medium-hunger conditions put in an appearance at their individual experimental rooms, they were not, of course, fed but they were handed the cookbook and given precisely the same instructions about the necessity for knowing the kinds of foods they eat.

Hunger was manipulated in this fashion in order to rule out the possible artifactual effects that the process of starvation itself might have on the experimental results; e.g., subjects who had gone without food might feel very differently about the experiment and their role in it and be much more eager to talk about the experiment than subjects who had eaten normally. Thus, both high- and low-hunger subjects went without food for approximately 20 hours and differed only in that low-hunger subjects were fed immediately before the experiment proper. Medium-hunger subjects, of course, went without food for only some six hours. In all other respects, the pre-experimental situations for the three sets of subjects were identical. The cookbook bit was introduced only as a means of keeping all subjects sensibly occupied while they waited alone for the experiment to begin. It was necessary to feed the low-hunger subjects in private and since we knew nothing at all as to what effect waiting alone in a strange room for some twenty minutes might have on experimental results, it seemed wisest to insure that this feature, too, was constant for all conditions.

The subjects remained in these rooms for approximately 20 to 25 minutes and were then assembled in a larger experimental room. There were always four subjects in each group—one from each of the three conditions and a fourth whose state of hunger was systematically rotated among the three conditions. For a few groups it was possible to get only three subjects and a stooge was used to fill up the group. The subjects were brought to the general experimental room one at a time, and while they waited for the experiment to begin they were asked to fill out a questionnaire containing numerous autobiographical questions and questions about food preferences. Again, this device was used to prevent the subjects from talking to one another.

Subjects assembled, the experimenter introduced himself and began:

> I want to thank you all again for coming today and for agreeing to go without food for as long a period as you have. As you know, our experiment today is concerned with the effects of particular kinds of food deprivation on the sensations. Specifically we shall be concerned with giving each of you various tests of your vision and hearing. Though these studies are of theoretical interest to us, I think also you will agree that they are of immediate practical importance as well. Food deprivation of one sort or another is fairly common today—in the

Orient, in Africa, in South America; and, though there have been many studies of the effects of food deprivation, we still, of course, have much to learn. As you might guess, these studies are also of potential interest and importance to the military, for, in combat, soldiers are frequently forced to go through prolonged periods on very limited or restricted rations and it is still an open question as to what are the precise effects of various kinds of rations.

Now I'd like to explain to you exactly what we will be doing. We are conducting four tests. Two of them are tests of vision and two are tests of hearing. Our apparatus is spread around on this floor and we conduct each of the tests in a different room. Each of you will be able to take only one test, since each of these tests requires about 35 minutes to administer. Now we need subjects in each of these tests and it does not matter to us which of the tests you individually take. And, since you've all been so good about coming today we'd like very much to give you freedom of choice to take whichever test interests you most. I've listed the names of these four tests on the board.

The experimenter reads off the names of the tests while he calls the subjects' attention to a blackboard on which the following is written:

Test	Sense Modality	Adaptation Period
1. Binocular Redundancy	Vision	Together with another Subject
2. Visual Diplacity	Vision	Alone
3. Auditory Peripherality	Hearing	Together with another Subject
4. Aural Angular Displacement	Hearing	Alone

He continues:

Now if you don't mind, I would prefer at this point not to describe the tests in any great detail. They're highly technical and it would require too much time now to explain them in full detail. Let me, however, say this much—two of these tests, binocular redundancy and visual diplacity, are tests of the visual sense. Two of the tests, auditory peripherality and aural angular displacement, are tests of hearing. Each test is administered in a separate room. Each test will require a ten-minute period of adaptation—that is, for a ten-minute period immediately before you take the test of your choice, we will put you in another room where we will ask you to wait under constant and controlled conditions for a ten-minute period.

For two of these tests, visual diplacity and aural angular displacement, it will be necessary that you spend this ten-minute adaptation period alone. For the test of visual diplacity it is necessary that no moving objects be in your field of vision. For the test of aural angular displacement, it is necessary that you be exposed to a minimum of extraneous sound. If you choose either of these tests, then, we will ask you to spend the ten-minute adaptation period alone.

If you choose either of the other two tests, binocular redundancy or auditory peripherality, you will, of course, also have a ten-minute adaptation period, but we will ask you to spend this period together with another subject. You may of course talk or do anything else you like during this time. When the adaptation period is over we will take you each to the proper testing room where you will be tested in private.

The experimenter then briefly reviewed all he had said and passed out sheets on which were printed the names of the tests, the sense modality that each tested, and the nature of the adaptation period required for each test. The experimenter asked the subjects to rate each test and to "please write the words 'most like' next to the name of the test you would most like to take. We will use this information to see that you take the test that interests you most."

This much done, the subjects were asked to answer a questionnaire, irrelevant to present concerns, and the experimenter then embarrassedly explained that the experiment was over and that there would be no tests of hearing or vision. Before going into an explanation the experimenter handed each subject a piece of paper and asked them to "write down the name of the test you said you would 'most like' to take; then think back to what went through your mind when you decided to take that test and tell us, as exactly as possible, why you decided to take that particular test, what factors made you decide the way you did." The entire experiment was then explained in detail, those who hadn't eaten were fed lavishly and fussed over, and all were sworn to secrecy. Before leaving, each subject filled out a brief questionnaire indicating whether he knew any of the other subjects present. None of the subjects knew other subjects in their groups beforehand.

The measure of the affiliative tendency is, of course, which of the tests the subjects indicated they would most like to take. The names of the tests are nothing but plausible-sounding nonsense syllables which could have no real meaning to the subjects, who made their choices largely in terms of the sense modality and the social or asocial nature of the adaptation period. Since there were two tests for each modality, if a subject preferred either vision or hearing he still chose between a "Together" and an "Alone" alternative.

RESULTS

The nature of the relationship between hunger and the affiliative tendency is indicated in Table 30. In the column labeled "Together" is recorded the number of subjects in each condition who wanted most to take one of the tests whose adaptation period would be spent with another subject. The column headed "Alone" includes all subjects who preferred taking a test whose adaptation period required being alone. In the high-hunger condition 67 percent of the subjects preferred one of the "Together" alternatives; in medium hunger, 35 percent; and in low hunger 30 percent. Hunger appears to be similar to anxiety; for both there is a positive relationship with the affiliative tendency.

Further support for this relationship comes from a more detailed consideration of the determinants of these choices. A choice of a "Together" alternative could be made either because the individual wants to be with people or because of some specific interest in this particular test. A choice of an "Alone" alternative could be made because the individual wants to avoid being with people or,

TABLE 30

RELATIONSHIP OF HUNGER TO THE AFFILIATIVE TENDENCY

	No. of subjects preferring to be:	
	Together	Alone
High Hunger	14	7
Medium Hunger	7	13
Low Hunger..........	6	14

$$X^2 = 6.62$$
$$d.f. = 2$$
$$.02 < p < .05$$

again, because of interest in the specific test. If the data already presented are a true reflection of a relationship between hunger and the affiliative tendency, it should be expected that, considering all subjects who made "Together" choices, the hungrier the subject the more salient the social motive. Conversely, for those subjects choosing "Alone" it should be anticipated that the hungrier the subject the more likely it is that his choice has been determined by an interest in a specific test rather than by antisocial feelings. It will be recalled that immediately after the subjects were told that the experiment was over, they were asked to write down why they had chosen as they did. Because of the structure of the tests, almost all of these reasons fall into one or both of the following categories:

1. A specific interest in the sense modality or an idiosyncratic interest in or interpretation of one of the four tests. Typical examples are: "I didn't know just exactly what the test was going to do, but I did think as long as it had something to do with hearing, I would be listening to possibly many different sounds. Another reason for the hearing test was because I have been using my eyes studying all morning and thought I would like to use my ears instead." "The reason I picked binocular redundancy is because the term redundancy is one that I am acquainted with. I had a high-school English teacher whose favorite word was redundancy. He used it too frequently, and it thus left an impression on me. I wanted to see just what Binocular Redundancy would be."

2. Socially relevant reasons. These include direct statements of a desire to be with other people and equally direct statements of a distaste for being with other people. Examples of social reasons are: "I wanted to spend the ten minutes in the company of one of the other people" and "I chose an experiment where I could first talk to someone as I felt like talking right then." Examples of antisocial reasons are: "I did not choose the other visual test because I did not want to spend ten minutes with one of these strangers" and "The fact that I would be alone before the thing started attracted me because I like to be alone, rather than make trivial conversation, etc., for a certain amount of time."

In addition to these two categories a few subjects indicated that it didn't make any difference at all to them and that they had chosen pretty much at random.

The distribution of these categories as they relate to choice and condition is presented in Table 31. This table is divided into two sub-tables: on the left are tabulated data for subjects who chose a "Together" test; on the right, the data for subjects who chose an "Alone" test. Some subjects gave only one reason for their choice, others gave several. If, no matter how many reasons a subject gave, one reason was either clearly social or antisocial, such a subject was tallied in the appropriate column labeled "Social Reasons" or "Antisocial Reasons." If no socially relevant reason was given, the subject was tallied in the appropriate "Modality Reasons" column. Those few subjects who indicated that they had chosen at random are included in the "Modality" column.

Turning first to those subjects who had elected a "Together" test, it is evident that almost everyone in the High Hunger condition who chose "Together" did so for socially motivated reasons. Thus, 92 percent of "Together" choosers in the High Hunger condition did so for social reasons. This proportion decreases as hunger decreases—in the Medium Hunger condition 71 percent and in the Low Hunger condition 50 percent of subjects choosing a "Together" alternative did so for social reasons.

Considering the "Alone" choosers, it is evident that the very

TABLE 31

REASONS GIVEN FOR CHOICE IN HUNGER-AFFILIATION EXPERIMENT

	No. of Subjects choosing a "Together" test who gave:		*No. of Subjects choosing an "Alone" test who gave:*	
	Social Reasons	*Modality Reasons*	*Antisocial Reasons*	*Modality Reasons*
High Hunger*	12	1	1	6
Medium Hunger	5	2	4	9
Low Hunger	3	3	8	6

* One subject in the high-hunger condition wrote an unintelligible and uncategorizable set of reasons for his choice of a "Together" alternative. This case is not included in this tabulation.

hungry subjects who chose "Alone" did not do so for antisocial reasons but largely because of some interest in the specific test. Only 14 percent of the High Hunger subjects who chose an "Alone" test gave an antisocial reason for doing so. This proportion increases as hunger decreases, with 31 percent of Medium Hunger and 57 percent of Low Hunger subjects indicating antisocial reasons for choosing an "Alone" alternative.*

Not only, then, did the hungry subjects choose to be together more often than less hungry subjects, but the stated motives for

* The rather high proportion of Low Hunger subjects giving antisocial reasons does suggest the "Thanksgiving dinner social syndrome"—oversatisfied eaters who can think of nothing nicer than being quietly left alone. This suggests, of course, the alternative interpretation that this pattern of experimental results is due to satiation. Though such an argument could be made for those subjects who had just eaten, it certainly cannot explain the results of the Medium Hunger subjects who chose "Together" alternatives significantly less often than High Hunger subjects and only slightly more often than Low Hunger subjects. These subjects had eaten only their normal breakfasts and at the time of the experiment had been without food for approximately 5 to 6 hours.

these choices are quite different for the various experimental groups. Choices of "Together" are determined by social motives to a greater extent for very hungry than for less hungry subjects. Social needs determined the choice of 57 percent of the High Hunger subjects and of only 15 percent of the Low Hunger subjects. Antisocial reasons account for a majority of the "Alone" choices of the Low Hunger group, while all but one of the "Alone" choices of the High Hunger group are determined by some idiosyncratic interest in the specific test. Antisocial feelings affected the choices made by 40 percent of the Low Hunger subjects and of less than 5 percent of the High Hunger subjects.

What about ordinal position? Though the number of cases available for this sub-analysis is quite small, there are no indications of even budding similarity to the data on the effects of ordinal position on the affiliative response to anxiety. With slight variation, first-born and later-born subjects chose the "Together" alternatives in roughly similar proportions in each of the experimental conditions considered separately. Whether or not to consider this finding as inconsistent with earlier results depends, of course, on the final interpretation of this entire body of data, a matter to which our final chapter will be devoted. In terms of the initial formulation which led to this particular study, a tentative conclusion of no relationship would not seem to be either disconcerting or particularly enlightening, for the most exotic sort of reasoning would be required to argue that parents are differentially hunger reducing or that, as may very well be the case with anxiety, first-borns are hunger increasers for their later-born siblings. It should be anticipated, however, that were hunger to be accompanied by true anxiety (as is undoubtedly the case in a famine situation where there is no clear possibility of getting food at any time), symptoms of differential dependence would be manifested.

DISCUSSION

Before returning to the theoretical issue from which this study evolved, we should like to examine the relationships of these experimental data to what little is known about the social consequences of hunger. Torrance (51) has surveyed relevant autobiographical reports and summarizes this material as follows: "Apparently, and this has been confirmed by observations in simulated survival situations, food deprivation is a stress which places a severe test upon group cohesiveness. While there are a few reports which tell of the sacrifices made by individuals for the communal effort, most survivors report disruptive effects on interpersonal relations in groups subjected to food deprivation. Particularly disruptive were those who betrayed the group to the enemy for food, those who stole food from their comrades, and mess personnel who worked in isolation from the group or who formed cliques."

Autobiographical reports, then, tend to indicate that hunger has disruptive effects on social relationships. Should the tenor of these reports be considered incompatible with the experimental results? Two hypotheses that may reconcile these apparently divergent data suggest themselves: (1) the relationship between hunger and the affiliative tendency may be a curvilinear one, so that at extremes of hunger the affiliative tendency decreases; (2) the real-life situation of being "Together" under conditions of deprivation is of course far more complex than the experimental "Together" situation, for which an attempt was deliberately made to eliminate all of the variables and complexities that might affect the relationship under test. By complexities we refer here to such matters as the obvious fact that in real life the presence of other people, with whom food must be shared, automatically limits one's own consumption and that the physical debility consequent on starvation may result in a state wherein the individual is almost ashamed to be with others. That some such factor as this last does operate is suggested by the preliminary results of an early version of the experiment described in this chapter. This earlier version followed precisely the procedure already described except for one crucial factor—in place of the innocent-sounding adaptation period, the tests themselves were to be taken alone or together with one other subject. Only a dozen or so trial subjects were run in this preliminary form of the experiment but there were strong indications that the pattern of the relationship was quite different, with proportionately fewer of the High Hunger subjects choosing a "Together" alternative. In stating the reasons for their choice, most of the very hungry subjects indicated that they had interpreted the "Together" alternatives as competitive situations, that because of doing without food, they did not feel physically up to par and that they wanted to avoid a competitive situation where they anticipated doing poorly.

This experiment was undertaken originally in an attempt to delineate the nature of the variables affecting the affiliative tendency. Though it would be satisfying on the basis of this study to be able to conclude that the affiliative tendency is a positively increasing function of drive state, sober consideration precludes any such sweeping conclusion, for it is possible that both anxiety and hunger are cross-cut by dimensions of discomfort, of tension, and of emotion. And, though we have investigated only the effects of states of psychological disturbance on affiliative behavior, it would not be too surprising eventually to discover that the affiliative tendency also increases with joy. Though we shall return to a more detailed consideration of this entire matter in the following chapters, it seems clear that considerably more work will be necessary before one can feel really confident about any conclusion more general than that affiliative tendencies increase with increasing anxiety and increasing hunger.

8

Anxiety Reduction and Self-Evaluation

Let us recapitulate the major findings of the studies presented thus far:

1. The affiliative tendency is positively related to the states of anxiety and hunger.

2. The relationship between anxiety and the affiliative tendency is independent of the opportunity to communicate, for it remains positive in a variety of conditions ranging from completely free communication to absolutely no verbal communication.

3. The affiliative tendency is highly directional. Anxious subjects want to be only with those in a similar plight.

4. There are individual differences in the propensity to affiliate under conditions of anxiety—a patent truism, but a remarkably effective discriminator is ordinal position of birth.

The interpretive implications of this series of findings have left us with two possible interpretations of the basic relationship between anxiety and the affiliative tendency. Under conditions of anxiety, the choice of "Together" is prompted by needs for anxiety reduction or by self-evaluative needs, or both. These alternatives, though initially plausible, are in a sense residual interpretations, for they are the explanatory possibilities remaining after a series of analytic experiments has ruled out the major alternative explanations. However, both of these residual interpretations have clear-cut implications of their own which permit direct testing of their explanatory power. If the presumed anxiety-reducing property of group membership is a potent determinant of the choice of "Together," it should be anticipated that being with others will actually reduce anxiety. If evaluative needs are major determinants of the relationship between anxiety and affiliation, it should be anticipated that being with others will lead to homogeneity of emotional intensity among the group members and to relative stability of emotion. This expectation derives from the set of assumptions, briefly discussed in the introductory chapter of this monograph, which indicate that social evaluation is possible only when there is relative homogeneity among the members of a reference group. Assuming evaluative needs and granting a situation in which evaluation is possible only through social comparison processes, it follows from the above that if discrepancies exist among group members, pressures will arise to reduce such discrepancy. If both the evaluative and anxiety-reducing alternatives are operative, it should be anticipated that under anxiety-producing conditions being together with others will lead to both anxiety reduction and relative homogeneity of anxiety intensity.

In order to test these several alternatives, Wrightsman (59) designed and conducted an experiment in which he experimentally produced a state of anxiety and then varied the social surroundings of his subjects. In some conditions, subjects were brought together to wait on their participation in the anxiety-provoking experiment; in a comparison condition, subjects waited in complete isolation. In this study, four subjects, previously unacquainted, were scheduled for each experimental group. As each subject arrived, he or she was met by a female assistant dressed as a nurse who showed each subject to a completely private room. In his own room, the subject was seated at a sterile-looking table on which was arrayed a variety of hypodermic needles, cotton swabs, alcohol, medicine bottles, slides, ampules, and syringes. The subject seated, the nurse asked him to fill out a brief questionnaire and told him that he would receive information about the experiment via the loudspeaker in his room. She then left the room, leaving the subject completely alone. In a few minutes, the loudspeaker in each room opened up with a tape-recorded talk, the essential features of which are the following:

> We have asked you to come today to serve as a subject in an experiment concerned with the relation of glucose level to the

efficiency of mental activity. . . . Briefly, what we will do is to drastically change the level of glucose in your blood, to see how this changes your ability to solve mental problems and tasks. The normal supply of glucose carried in the blood is around sixty to ninety milligrams per hundred cubic centimeters of blood. First we will take a blood sample from you to determine just how much we can change the glucose level and still avoid harmful effects or damaging results. This sample need be only a drop of blood and it will be collected by pricking your finger. This sample will be placed under a microscope for a quick check of the approximate glucose level. Then we will change your glucose level. In some cases we will raise it upward, by injection of a glucose-additive. In other cases we will lower the glucose level through the use of a drug which serves as a glucose-depressant.

As we want to test the immediate effects of change in glucose-level on how you react to a series of problems that follow, it is necessary for us to administer the depressant-drug and glucose-additive in a manner that gets the substance into the blood and the cells as quickly as possible. Therefore we will give you an injection or a series of injections of about one and one-half cubic centimeters with a hypodermic needle. These will be administered to you so that they enter the bloodstream immediately and because of this they are likely to be more painful than routine injections. Only a nurse or technician will be present with you during the injection period.

Although I can't tell you much more about the experiment, in all fairness I should warn you that the injection of the drug will cause you to feel drowsy and lacking in energy—sort of slowed down or a "woozy" feeling—but you should be able to maintain your ability to respond. With some subjects such a feeling may be maintained for several hours before passing away. If your glucose level is raised, the new concentration will be abnormally high, at an absolute maximum amount near the point which brings on glucose-shock, fainting, and similar symptoms of hyperglycemia or diabetes. But such changes, if they occur, will cause no permanent harm.

Before beginning, we have a set of questions which we

would like you to answer. When you get your copy, please write your name at the top of the first sheet, read the directions carefully, and give the most accurate answer you can to each question. Thank you.

Following this, a brief questionnaire was distributed to all subjects with the rationale that it was necessary to get additional information about the subjects in order to understand their reactions during the experiment. The chief item on this questionnaire was a question designed to measure anxiety level which read:

> For normative purposes, the research committee would like you to indicate just how at-ease or ill-at-ease you feel about being a subject in an experiment involving the taking of a blood test and hypodermic injection and involving changes in one's physiological state.
>
> Please assign a number anywhere from 0 to 100 to indicate your feeling. The number 0 would indicate that you felt completely at-ease and felt no concern over having a blood test and a drug-injection and participating in the experiment. The number 100 would indicate that you felt extremely ill-at-ease and were very concerned about taking a blood test and injection and participating in this experiment. You may choose any number from 0 through 100.

This question answered, the subjects were assigned to one of the three experimental conditions—"Alone," "Together Talk," or "Together No-Talk."

Alone. When a subject had answered this last question, the nurse reentered the room, collected the questionnaire, and simply said, "You are to wait here till we are ready to use you. You can study or read or smoke if you like. There will be only a short wait." The nurse then left the room, leaving the subject completely alone for five minutes. In this condition, then, there are four subjects, each in a private room and having no contact with one another, each exposed at the same time to the same anxiety-provoking instructions and each awaiting injection in isolation.

Together Talk. Having answered the questionnaire, all four subjects were brought together in a common room and told, "You are to wait here until we are ready to use you. You can study or read or smoke if you like. If you want to talk, that's okay. You can talk about the experiment or anything you like. There will be only a short wait." The experimenter and nurse then left the room for a five-minute period. During this five-minute period the group was observed through a one-way mirror.

Together No-Talk. All four subjects were brought together in a common room and told, "You are to wait here until we are ready to use you. You can study or read or smoke if you like. However, please do *not* talk. Part of the experiment is of a verbal nature and we want only your own ideas to be given. Therefore it is important that you not talk about the experiment or anything else. There will be only a short wait." And again the experimenters left the room for a five-minute period and observed the group during this time. All groups obeyed these "no-talk" instructions completely.

After this five-minute wait, the subjects in all conditions were told that the experiment was about to begin and were asked to fill out a final questionnaire designed again to measure anxiety level. The chief items of this questionnaire were the following:

1. A repetition of the measure already described in which the subjects are asked to estimate their degree of uneasiness on a 0–100 point scale.

2. The "Anx 2" measurement described in Chapter 4. This is a six-point scale ranging from "1. I feel completely calm" to "6. I feel extremely uneasy" in response to the question, "How nervous and uneasy do you feel about taking part in this experiment involving hypodermic injections?"

3. Finally, the subjects were given the option of deciding for themselves whether or not they wished to take part in the experiment. Again, the question was similar in form to that used in the experiments described in earlier chapters.

These questions answered, the experiment was over and an explanation and catharsis session ensued.

In each condition there was a total of seventeen groups, each consisting of four subjects. In each condition there was a total of

TABLE 32

EFFECTS OF BEING ALONE OR WITH OTHERS ON ANXIETY

Condition	No. of Groups	No. of Subjects	Anx 2	% Subjects refusing to continue	Pre-waiting-period Index	Post-waiting-period Index	Changes in Anx Pre-Post Index
Alone	17	68	2.79	14.9	41.35	37.16	−4.19
Together No-Talk	17	68	2.91	8.8	42.76	36.59	−6.17
Together Talk ..	17	68	2.85	14.7	43.69	37.26	−6.43

seven all-male groups and ten all-female groups. All subjects were psychology student volunteers, receiving extra course credit for participation in the experiment. In all of the data to be presented, the trends revealed are precisely the same for male and female groups and the data from the two sets of groups will be pooled in all tables.

ANXIETY REDUCTION

If the anxiety-reduction hypothesis is correct, it should be anticipated that there will be greater anxiety reduction in the "Together" conditions than in the "Alone" condition. Table 32 presents the relevant data. It should be noted first that the groups are similar in their initial level of anxiety. Scores on the pre-waiting-period index (the first measure requiring the subjects to estimate their degree of uneasiness on a 0–100 point scale) are much the same in the three conditions. And following the experimental treatments the picture remains much the same: though there is a general trend to anxiety reduction with time, the terminal level of anxiety is almost identical in the three conditions. For none of the measures does any of the possible between-condition comparisons even approach statistical significance. It would appear that being with others has no particular anxiety-reducing effect.

It will be recalled, however, that in the earlier experiments the relationship between anxiety and the affiliative tendency was restricted almost entirely to subjects who were first-born and only children. It is reasonable, then, to suggest that anxiety reduction, if indeed it is a consequence of being with others, would be stronger for early- than for later-born subjects. Such an effect could, of course, be obscured in the data presented in Table 32, which lumps together the data of all subjects. The data for the two sets of subjects are presented separately in Table 33. For tabular convenience, this table presents only the data gathered in the pre- and post-waiting-period administrations of the 0–100 point scale of "uneasiness." Data on the remaining two measures are presented in the footnote on page 113. It should be noted now, however, that the trends are precisely the same on all measures of anxiety.

TABLE 33

RELATIONSHIP OF ORDINAL POSITION TO ANXIETY REDUCTION

Condition	N	First-born and only Subjects				N	Later-born Subjects				First vs. Later P value*	
		Pre-waiting period index	Post-waiting period index	Anxiety reduction pre-post indices	Gross change		Pre-waiting period index	Post-waiting period index	Anxiety reduction pre-post indices	Gross change	Anxiety reduction	Gross change
Alone†	41	42.07	38.56	−3.51	4.24	26	39.89	35.42	−4.47	6.00	n.s.	n.s.
TNT	33	43.24	33.91	−9.33	9.94	35	42.37	39.11	−3.26	4.17	.06	.07
TT†	32	39.81	31.47	−8.34	10.84	35	47.77	42.91	−4.86	6.57	n.s.	.05
P value*												
Alone vs. TNT				<.05	<.05				n.s.	n.s.		
P value												
Alone vs. TT				<.05	<.01				n.s.	n.s.		

* All levels of confidence computed by the Mann-Whitney U test.
† The total N in these conditions is slightly smaller than in Table 32 owing to the elimination of twins and adopted children.

The columns in Table 33 labeled "Anxiety Reduction" contain the algebraic means of the changes in anxiety level from pre- to post-waiting-period administrations of the uneasiness measure. The minus sign, of course, indicates a decrease of anxiety. It will be noted immediately that there is greater anxiety reduction for first-born subjects in the "Together" conditions than for first-born subjects in the "Alone" condition. No such effect is evident for later-born subjects for whom the degree of anxiety reduction seems much the same in the three experimental conditions. It would appear, then, that being with others does have anxiety-reducing effects for first-born and only subjects. This finding, of course, agrees neatly with the consistent tendency, in the earlier experiments, for anxious first-born subjects to choose "Together." This pair of complementing facts gives strong support to the hypothesis that one of the determinants of the "Together" choice is the anxiety-reducing property of being with other people.

The relationship at issue, however, may not be quite as simple as the last paragraph would indicate. The columns labeled "Gross Change" in Table 33 contain the arithmetic means of the changes in anxiety level. These figures represent the absolute magnitude of change, regardless of whether a change indicates anxiety reduction or increase. Again, first-borns in "Together" conditions change considerably more than do first-borns in the "Alone" condition. And again there are no between-condition differences of any consequence among the later-born subjects. It should be noted, however, that while anxiety reduction is greatest in the "Together No-Talk" condition, gross change is greatest in the "Together Talk" condition. Comparison of the magnitude of the two sets of scores would indicate that the gross change in the "Together No-Talk" condition is made up of anxiety-reducing scores to a somewhat greater extent than in the "Together Talk" condition. Furthermore, it should be noted, on the right-hand side of the table, that when first- and later-borns *within* the "Together Talk" condition are compared, the two groups differ significantly in gross change but not in anxiety reduction. Though certainly the magnitudes of the differences in the several comparisons just made are not great, they do at least suggest that for first-borns in the "Together Talk" condition, anxiety reduction is not an inevitable consequence of being with others. First-born subjects, as suggested by the gross-change data, are more influencible than later-born subjects. If the tenor of a group discussion were to be really terrifying and anxiety provoking, it might indeed be anticipated that the anxiety of first-borns would be greater than that of later-borns.

Let us summarize these findings so far. For first-born subjects, anxiety reduction is a consequence of being together with other people in a similar plight. For such subjects, the simple physical presence of other people, as in the "pure" "Together No-Talk" condition, is anxiety reducing. Allowing the subjects to communicate with one another may somewhat complicate the relationship, for first-born subjects are more influencible than later-born subjects. It is suggested that when communication is allowed, the effect on anxiety of being with others will depend on the nature of the communication.*

* In order not to depart, within the body of the text, from the main themes of this chapter, we have delayed to this footnote the examination of Wrightsman's data for additional evidence on the relationship of ordinal position to the level of anxiety or fear. The earlier experiments have consistently indicated that, in standard fear-provoking situations, first-born subjects are more frightened than later-born subjects. Wrightsman's experiment yields results that are partially inconsistent with these earlier findings. In Table 33, the columns labeled "Pre-waiting-period index" provide an indication of the degree of anxiety immediately after the "injection" instructions and before the experimental treatment involving waiting alone or with others. Comparison of the relevant columns reveals that first-born subjects were slightly more frightened than later-born subjects in the "Alone" and "Together No-Talk" conditions but quite a bit less frightened in the "Together Talk" condition. The combined data of the three conditions yield a slightly higher score for later-born than for early-born subjects. However, data obtained with the "Anx 2" and "Percent of Subjects refusing to continue" measures are quite consistent with the earlier findings. Though we present below the data for all three conditions, it must be remembered that only the data for the "Alone" condition are relevant to the

THE SOCIAL EVALUATION OF ANXIETY

Before examining Wrightsman's data for indications of social evaluation of anxiety, let us review the scheme evolved (15) from the large number of studies on social determinants of opinion and ability evaluation. It has been hypothesized, first, that a drive exists in man to evaluate his opinions and abilities, i.e., to determine the "rightness" or "wrongness" of an opinion and the "goodness" or "badness" of an ability. Secondly, it is hypothesized that when an objective, nonsocial means (e.g., a reality check or reference to an authoritative source) of evaluation is not available, evaluation will be made by comparison with the opinions and abilities of other people. Finally, it is hypothesized that stable and precise evaluation by social comparison is possible only when the opinions and abilities available for comparison are not too divergent from one's own; the tendency to compare oneself with others decreases as the discrepancy in opinion or ability increases.

From these several hypotheses it may be derived that when dis-

---

point at issue. Both of these measures were administered only *after* the waiting period. It has been demonstrated above that in the "Together" conditions, following the waiting period, anxiety reduction is greater for first-born than for later-born subjects. Most plausibly, then, the scores on these measures in the two "Together" conditions should be higher for later-born than for early-born subjects.

	First-born and only Subjects			*Later-born Subjects*		
Condition	*N*	*Anx 2*	*% S's re-fusing to continue*	*N*	*Anx 2*	*% S's re-fusing to continue*
Alone	41	2.95	22.0	26	2.58	3.9
TNT	33	2.76	6.1	35	3.06	11.4
TT	32	2.69	12.5	35	3.00	17.1

Though the differences are not as marked as in the early experiments, it will be seen that in the "Alone" condition first-born subjects are quite a bit more anxious than later-born subjects by both measures. We must admit that we are somewhat at a loss to explain this incon-

crepancies of opinion or abilities exist among the members of a group, pressures will arise to reduce such discrepancies. In interpersonal settings, such pressures to uniformity can be manifested in three ways. When discrepancies exist, tendencies will arise to: (1) change one's own opinion or ability to bring oneself closer to other group members; (2) change others in the group so as to bring them closer to oneself; and (3) cause one to cease comparing oneself to those in the group who are extremely different from oneself. This schema has proven particularly useful in understanding social determinants of opinion and ability evaluation, and numerous experiments have demonstrated the operation of these tendencies as they relate to such variables as degree of discrepancy, cohesiveness, and importance of issue.

Now if the suggestion that the emotions, like the opinions and abilities, are evaluated by means of social comparison processes is

---

sistent pattern of results, for unless one were willing to defend some utterly far-fetched notion such as a first-born's antipathy to high numbers, no hypothesis readily suggests itself to explain these results. This much, however, is clear: on the two measures common to all of the experiments the differences between first- and later-born subjects are consistent; with the new measure there is no difference between the two groups. The explanation may lie in the nature of this new measure, in the different manipulations of anxiety, or, most reasonably, in the generally lower level of anxiety produced in this experiment as compared with the earlier experiments. It will be recalled (Table 14) that in the low-anxiety conditions of the earlier experiments there were no differences between early- and later-born subjects. In the high-anxiety conditions of these earlier experiments, all subjects averaged 3.61 on the "Anx 2" measure while Wrightsman's subjects in the "Alone" condition averaged 2.81 on this same measure—a substantial and highly significant difference. It may be, then, that this new uneasiness measure is not particularly at fault but that these particular differences between first- and later-born subjects will manifest themselves strongly and on all measures only when anxiety is extreme. Whatever the explanation, it is clear that more work will be required before one can have full confidence in the replicability of these particular results for the relationship of ordinal position to fear.

correct, it should be anticipated that these same manifestations of pressures to uniformity will be evident in situations where discrepancies of emotional state exist. In such situations, too, there should be indications of self change, of attempts to influence others and bring them closer to one's own position, and of the rejection, as comparison points, of those who deviate too far from one's own position. In the brief discussion of "gross change" which terminated the preceding section of this chapter, it was suggested that the relatively large gross change in the "Together Talk" condition was an indication of on-going social influence. But, let us ask first, do such changes really indicate influencibility or are they merely random changes suggesting that people are simply more flighty when in one another's presence than when they are alone? If random "flightiness" is the appropriate explanation, no particular change in the final as compared with the initial dispersion of scores on the "0 to 100 uneasiness" scale should be anticipated; if influencibility is the proper explanation, it should be expected that the final scores on this scale will be more homogeneous than the initial scores, for presumably people are being influenced toward one another's position—and this, of course, is precisely the result that the self-evaluation schema demands, for the effects of tendencies to bring oneself into closer conformity to others and to influence others to closer agreement with oneself would necessarily result in homogenization of emotional state.

As an index of the degree of homogenization in each group, the range of scores on post-waiting-period administration of the "0 to 100" point scale is simply divided by the range of scores in the pre-waiting-period administration of this same scale. For example, a group of subjects who before the waiting period gave scores of 40, 60, 80, and 90 and after the waiting period scores of 45, 60, 70, and 85 would have an index of .80. The lower the score, the greater the degree of social influence and homogenization.

Data derived from these computations are presented in Table 34. The indices of homogenization for both "Together" conditions are noticeably smaller than the figure obtained for the "Alone" condition. These decreases in dispersion are significantly smaller than 1.00 (the point at which the initial and final ranges are identical) at the .01 level for "Together Talk" and the .02 level of confidence for the "Together No-Talk" condition. The fact that both "Together" conditions differ significantly from the "Alone" condition is an indication that this decrease in dispersion is not a result of some pure artifact such as a tendency for those who initially chose extreme scores to be more moderate in their second judgment.

TABLE 34

EFFECT OF BEING WITH OTHERS ON HOMOGENIZATION OF ANXIETY

Condition	N	Mean Initial Range	Mean Index of Homogenization
Alone	17	67.06	.980
TNT	17	65.29	.841
TT	17	66.65	.831
		TT vs. Alone:	$t = 2.37$
			$p = .03$
		TNT vs. Alone:	$t = 2.08$
			$p = .05$

It would certainly appear, then, that social influence does take place and that homogenization of anxiety is a clear consequence of being with others. The fact that the "Together No-Talk" index is almost as low as the "Together Talk" index could lead one to speculation about self-evaluative needs and pressures to uniformity so great that subjects soundlessly search out and accommodate to cues as to how others are responding; or it could lead to a search for an artifact. And one possible artifact does suggest itself from the fact that the measure used has zero as a built-in floor and that there is a general tendency for anxiety to decrease with time, with the "Together" groups decreasing overall slightly more than the "Alone" groups. This combination of factors might lead to lower indices of homogenization in the "Together" conditions. If such an artifact is at work, it should be expected that there will be a sizeable correlation between the magnitude of anxiety decrease and the index of homogenization. Examination of the "Together Talk" data makes it clear that such an artifact has at best a trivial impact. In this condition some groups increase in anxiety level and other groups decrease. The changes in anxiety level vary from a mean increase of 5.00 to a decrease of 26.75, and there is only a small and nonsignificant correlation between the magnitude of anxiety decrease and the index of homogenization. In the "Together No-Talk" groups, on the other hand, there is fairly consistent decrease of anxiety level in all groups (mean change varies from 0 to a decrease of 18.75) and the correlation between anxiety reduction and homogenization is $+.57$, significant at the .02 level of confidence. It may be concluded, then, that the decrease in dispersion in "Together Talk" groups is a result of social-influence processes, while a similar decrease in "Together No-Talk" groups is at least in part artifactually produced.

So far, in support of the suggestion that the emotions, like the opinons, are subject to social influence and evaluation, it has been demonstrated that emotional states of group members grow more alike as a result of interaction, an indication that, as with opinions and abilities, tendencies to self change and to influence others are active when discrepancies among group members exist.

Let us examine Wrightsman's experiment next for indications of the operation of the final tendency postulated—the tendency to cease comparison with those in the group who are extremely different from oneself. It has been hypothesized that the tendency to compare oneself with others decreases as the discrepancy increases. It should follow from this that in the "Together Talk" condition of this experiment, when the initial range of anxiety is great there should be relatively little change and little homogenization of state of anxiety, for in such groups discrepancy is so great that comparison may cease. Further, it should be anticipated, again in the

"Together Talk" condition, that when the initial range of scores is small there will be little change and little further homogenization, for when the discrepancy is small, evaluation is immediately possible and influence processes will cease. Only for intermediate ranges of discrepancy should there be strong indications of social influence and homogenization. It is anticipated, then, that in the "Together Talk" condition there will be a non-monotonic relationship, peaking at intermediate ranges, between the initial range of anxiety scores and the degree of homogenization.

In the "Alone" condition, there should of course be no relationship between initial range and degree of homogenization. Subjects in this condition are completely isolated and have no idea of how other people are reacting. There should therefore be little change and no homogenization no matter what the initial range of these arbitrarily designated "groups" of subjects.

For the "Together No-Talk" condition, it is of course impossible to make any clear-cut prediction. If the homogenization noted in Table 34 is largely a function of the artifact discussed, the relationship between initial range and homogenization should be simply an elevated version of the straight-line curve predicted for the "Alone" condition—roughly equal homogenization at all ranges of initial discrepancy. If, on the other hand, social comparison processes are really at work in this condition, the relationship at issue should resemble that in the "Together Talk" condition. Clearly, though, subjects in this condition could not have as clear a picture of their fellow subjects' emotional states as would subjects in the "Together Talk" condition, and it would therefore be reasonable to expect that, if social comparison processes are at work, the plotted relationship between range and homogenization will be somewhat flatter in the "Together No-Talk" than in the "Together Talk" condition, i.e., somewhat greater homogenization at the extreme ranges, somewhat lower peak at the intermediate ranges.

Data on this relationship are presented in Figure 2. Along the abscissa are plotted the ranges of scores obtained in the experimental groups on the first administration of the "0 to 100 uneasiness" scale. The range obtained in each group is assigned to one of three classifications: "wide" initial range where the distance between the least and most anxious member of the group is between 80 and 100; "intermediate" initial ranges where this distance is between 55 and 79; and "narrow" initial ranges where this distance falls between 0 and 54. These particular cut-off points were chosen simply because they are the points at which one can come closest to assigning 25 percent of the total number of groups to the "wide" range category and 25 percent of the total number of groups to the "narrow" range category. Along the ordinate is plotted the mean index of homogenization for the groups in each of the categories. At 1.00 there has been no decrease in dispersion from initial to final measure. The closer the index to zero, the greater the decrease in dispersion of scores from first to final measure.

It can be seen immediately in Figure 2 that the curves for the "Alone" and "Together Talk" groups follow expectations closely. In the "Alone" condition, clearly there is no indication of relationship between initial range and degree of homogenization. All points on the "Alone" curve are quite close to 1.00—the point at which there is no change in dispersion. The "Together Talk" curve, on the other hand, indicates a marked relationship between range and homogenization. For groups with both "wide" and "narrow" initial ranges, there is relatively little homogenization; "intermediate" range groups, on the other hand, markedly decrease dispersion from first to final measure of anxiety—precisely the pattern that the social comparison schema would lead us to expect. Neither wide- nor narrow-range groups on the "Together Talk" condition differ significantly from their counterparts in the "Alone" condition. "Together Talk" intermediate-range groups are significantly greater than similar "Alone" groups at better than the .05 level of confidence by Median Test. "Together Talk" intermediate-range groups are significantly greater than "Together

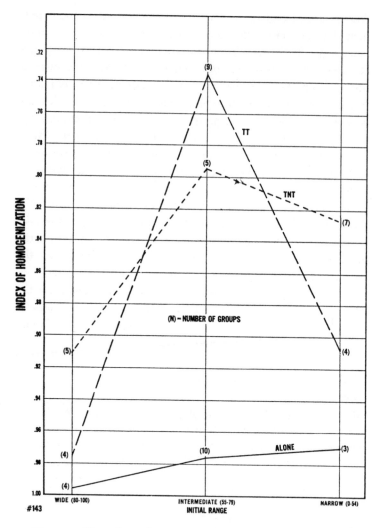

Figure 2. The effects of initial range on homogenization of anxiety.

Talk" extreme-range groups at better than the .05 level of confidence by the same test.* The "Together No-Talk" curve does appear as a somewhat flattened version of the "Together Talk" curve, which might be taken as a tentative indication of the operation of comparison processes in this condition. However, the points on this curve are not significantly different from one another, and though it is engaging to speculate about the possibility that social influence processes may be active even when subjects are limited to simple observation of one another, it is clear that such a hypothesis receives only tentative support within the present study.

Let us summarize this section. It has been hypothesized that the emotions, like the opinions and abilities, are evaluated by social comparison processes. The test of this hypothesis demands the demonstration that when discrepancies of emotional state exist among the members of a group, social influence and rejection processes are active. The decrease in discrepancy of anxiety states after a period of interaction in the "Together Talk" condition is evidence that social influence processes are operative. The failure

* Before concluding, on the basis of these data, that the tendency to cease comparing oneself with those who are extremely different is operating in the "Together Talk" condition of this experiment, one possibly confounding factor must be examined. Clearly the wide-range groups will almost inevitably contain relatively more subjects who chose extreme positions than will the intermediate-range groups. It is conceivable that such subjects, who are initially either extremely worried or very calm, are simply less influencible than subjects whose initial reaction is between these extremes. Whether or not this is a factor can be simply determined by comparing the change patterns of such extreme subjects in wide- and intermediate-range groups. If the noninfluencibility of extreme subjects is the proper explanation there should be no difference between the two groups of subjects. If the tendency to cease comparison is the proper explanation, wide-range-extreme subjects should change less than intermediate-range-extreme subjects. The data are presented in the table below, where subjects in the "Together Talk" condition whose initial score on the "0 to 100" scale fell between 75 and 100 are considered extreme high-anxiety subjects and those whose ini-

to reduce discrepancy in wide-range groups is an indication of rejection.

Wrightsman's experiment, then, indicates that both the anxiety-reduction and self-evaluation explanations of the anxiety-affiliation relationship demonstrated in earlier experiments have good experimental support. Being with others is anxiety reducing for first-born subjects, precisely the subjects who, when anxious, chose to be with others. Being with others leads to strong manifestations of social influence and rejection, precisely the consequences demanded by the assumption of a need for evaluation of emotional states. There is good reason to believe, then, that the prime motivators of the choice of "Together" when anxious are needs for anxiety reduction and for self-evaluation. However, though we have fair confidence that both of these needs, independent of each other, have positive relationships with the affiliative tendency, it

---

tial score was between 0 and 25 are classified as extreme low-anxiety subjects.

	Together Talk Wide-Range Groups		*Together Talk Intermediate-Range Groups*	
	N	Gross change	N	Gross change
Extreme high Anx (75–100)	5	6.00	9	17.22
Extreme low Anx (0–25)	10	3.00	13	9.23

Clearly, there is considerably less change among the extremes of wide-range groups than among the extremes of intermediate-range groups. It may be concluded, then, that the difference in homogenization between wide- and intermediate-range "Together Talk" groups in Figure 2 does result from the operation of the "tendency to cease comparison with deviates" rather than from any artifactual effect of the presumed unchangeability of extreme subjects.

In the "Together No-Talk" condition the pattern of data is much the same, though the differences between extreme subjects in wide- and intermediate-range groups are somewhat smaller than in the "Together Talk" condition.

is clear that only an experiment which separately manipulates these two needs can definitively establish the point.

SATIATION AND SOCIAL COMPARISON PROCESSES

It is of course tempting to treat the results of the experiment just discussed as generalizable to all emotional states but, so far, our conclusions must be restricted to the state of anxiety and, more specifically still, to the breed of anxiety generated by physical fear. Is there evidence that social-comparison processes affect other states of emotion or feeling? A study conducted by Horwitz, Exline, Goldman, and Lee (31) yields evidence on the state of satiation or boredom. This experiment was designed to study the effects of a variety of group characteristics on the rate of satiation of group members working on a repetitive group task. Experimental groups in this study consisted of five subjects seated around a table, all facing a common work area. By a system of partitions the subjects were prevented from seeing one another. Each subject was provided with a stick, and the group task consisted of the assembly, using these sticks, of an exceedingly simple jigsaw puzzle. In the center of the work area was placed a simple outline drawing of a locomotive marked off in five sections. Five jigsaw pieces, cut to fit each of these sections, were placed around the drawing and the group's job was to fill in the drawing with these pieces. After the drawing was filled in the experimenter separated the pieces and the group repeated the task. This procedure continued for each group until it had completed at least forty trials of precisely the same task and had worked at least eighty minutes.

After each trial the subjects privately checked off a scale designed to measure satiation. For this measure they answered the question, "How do you feel about doing this particular task again?" by choosing one of six points ranging from "*a.* I feel at least *some interest* in repeating this task," to "*f.* I feel that repeating the task is *intensely distasteful* to me."

This was a six-condition experiment. In five of the conditions, the experimental groups were made up of strangers. In a sixth condition, experimental groups were made up of people who knew one another. The experiment was introduced to all groups with the instructions, "There must be absolutely no talking during the test." The groups of strangers obeyed these instructions to the letter and went about their task in complete silence. Among the groups of acquaintances, however, restraints against making noise were apparently somewhat lower and communication of a sort did take place in such groups. In no case did this involve more than rudimentary conversation. The subjects in such groups simply used occasional expletives, or groaned, sighed, and the like—in short, made just the sort of noises that effectively convey a mood or feeling. For our purposes, then, this experiment involves two sets of groups—one in which the subjects can neither see nor hear one another and have flatly no idea of how others are reacting to the situation; another in which subjects can hear, though not see, one another and in all likelihood, therefore, have a fair idea of how other members of the group are reacting. If it is correct that the feelings and emotions are evaluated by comparison with others, it should be anticipated that, as with anxiety, the degree of satiation within those groups where this rudimentary sort of communication takes place should be more homogeneous than in groups where there is no such communication. And the data indicate that this is the case. In those groups where communication took place, the within-groups variance for satiation scores is .92, with 31 degrees of freedom. In groups where there was no communication, within-groups variance on satiation is 1.56, with 146 degrees of freedom. The F value is 1.70, which is significant at better than the .05 level of confidence. It would certainly appear, then, that these subjects have evaluated their own feelings of fatigue, annoyance, and satiation by reference to the cues they receive from other group members. This interpretation is somewhat confounded, of course, by the fact that in this experiment degree of friendship and degree of communication varied simultaneously. It does seem a fairly safe bet, however, that communication is the crucial variable.

It should be noted, too, that, as with anxiety, this opportunity to get cues had no systematic effect on the degree of satiation beyond drawing the members of the group closer together in their feelings. Some of these communicating groups maintained a high degree of interest throughout the experiment, whereas others satiated very quickly. The mean level of satiation was similar for the two sets of groups.

For both the states of anxiety and satiation, then, there is good evidence that social-influence processes are operative and that the individual evaluates his own feelings by comparing himself with others. It should be noted that in both of these experiments, there were no externally imposed pressures to uniformity. There was no group goal, no reward for conformity, and no penalty for non-conformity. The subjects, in both experiments, made their judgments of their own emotional states in complete privacy. In short, there is every indication that the conformity evidenced in both studies is a manifestation of a genuine individual need for appraisal of a state of emotion or feeling.

9

Social Determinants of Emotional State

Having investigated specific states of anxiety and satiation, let us attempt to fit these notions of social determination of emotional state into a more general formulation. What is known of the physiology of emotion seems to indicate no clear-cut differences in bodily state to distinguish among the variously labeled emotional states. Characteristically, emotional states are marked by bodily changes resulting from the activity of the autonomic nervous system but, with the possible exception of patterns of skeletal response in such states as startle, much research has failed to reveal clearly distinguishable physiological correlates for the various emotions. Woodworth and Schlosberg (58) introduce their review of research in this area as follows, "Psychologists and physiologists have made extensive investigations of many physiological functions in the hope that they would find some patterning to correspond to the common-sense distinctions among the various emotional states. We shall devote the next two chapters to their findings, but we may as well warn the reader now that he will discover very little evidence for differentiation among emotions when he looks inside the skin." (P. 133.) And yet our language is rich in terms designating a huge variety of supposedly distinct emotional states—a puzzle of sorts, and one which Woodworth and Marquis (57) discuss as follows, "The several emotions are distinguished, in practice, by stating the external situation in which each occurs and the type of overt response demanded. Any particular emotion is the stirred-up state appropriate to a certain situation and overt response." (P. 330.) "Appropriate"—an apt but odd choice of word, for just how does the emoter "decide" which is the appropriate state? Exactly what does determine whether a person will label his feelings as anger, vexation, impatience, or fury? Precisely this question has compelled most writers on the subject to define emotion in terms of both physiological and situational or cognitive factors. Thus, in two major treatises on emotion, we find Young (60) defining emotion as "an acute disturbance or upset of the individual which is revealed in behavior and in conscious experience, as well as through widespread changes in the functioning of viscera, and which is initiated by factors within a psychological situation" (p. 51); and Ruckmick (35) writing, "There is a tendency . . . to admit that pure bodily expression without the cognitive or 'intellectual' factor does not qualify as an equation for the experienced real emotion" (p. 343) and "we have learned that the feelings ultimately become involved with other mental processes, especially with the cognitive processes. What the child therefore feels depends more and more on what he cognizes or, in short, on the accumulations of his perceptual and ideational experiences" (p. 448).

All of which leaves us with cognitive factors as the determiners of the appropriateness of an emotion; that is, one labels, interprets, and identifies the stirred-up state characteristic of emotion in terms of the characteristics of the precipitating situation and of one's apperceptive mass. Without laboring the obvious, the immediate situation as interpreted by past experience furnishes the framework within which one understands and labels his own feelings. This formulation leaves us with precisely identifiable and understandable bodily and emotional states only when the precipitating situation is completely clear-cut and recognizable. And indeed the emotions precipitated by many situations *are* completely clear-cut. When we are faced with an armed holdup man, there is no ambiguity about either the situation or our feelings. A student who has just learned that he has failed an important examination has no problem in understanding his feelings. In both cases, one's experience and knowledge make the situation and one's reaction to the situation completely clear. But what of disturbing situations which are more ambiguous and unfamiliar? Consider, as a prime ex-

ample, the situation facing a subject in one of the high-anxiety
conditions of our anxiety-affiliation experiments. Partly out of
interest, partly to get extra class credit, a student volunteers to take
part in a psychological experiment. She comes at her appointed
hour to find herself surrounded by electrical apparatus, facing a
doctor who rather ominously tells her that she will be shocked—
an unexpected and unfamiliar situation. Without any doubt the
subject is disturbed and uneasy. But precisely what *does* she
or, perhaps, *should* she feel? What is the appropriate emotion?
Amusement at allowing herself to be trapped? Chagrin? Anger
at the experimenter? Anxiety and worry over the impending
shock and pain? And if anxiety, precisely how much anxiety—
terror or mild concern? The situation is such, then, that the subject, who is undoubtedly disturbed and stirred-up, has no precise
way of understanding or labeling her feelings and state of disturbance, no precise way of deciding her reaction.

We would suggest, of course, that the evaluative needs are maxi-
mally operative in such a situation. Just as there are pressures to
establish the "correctness" of an opinion and the "goodness" of an
ability, there are pressures to establish the "appropriateness" of an
emotion or bodily state. In the case of the opinions and abilities,
when there is no possibility of a physical check or a check against
authoritative sources, pressures arise to establish a social reality.
In the case of an emotion, when the precipitating situation is ambiguous or uninterpretable in terms of past experience, again
pressures arise to establish a social reality. And since emotion-
producing situations are often novel and outside the realm of our
past experience, it could be expected that the emotions would be
particularly vulnerable to social influence. It may be this presumed
vulnerability that will eventually help us understand phenomena
of emotional contagion such as panic and riots.

Clearly this brief treatment of emotion is simply a point of view
and one that is peculiarly marked with problems, some definitional,
some research, some both. For example, are we *really* talking about
emotion or are we talking about opinions of emotion? Do the

anxieties of the subjects in our experiments really vary in the conforming fashion described or is it simply a verbal statement about emotion that varies? At this point we are not even certain that the question is meaningful, but there are at least research possibilities, for a study in which one independently obtained verbal statements of felt anxiety and measures of presumed physiological correlates of anxiety (such as the psycho-galvanic skin response) should clarify the point. However, rather than, at this stage, worrying through problems that are better left for further research and analysis, let us examine the way in which the several studies reported in this volume tie in with this view of emotion.

Simply put, our major point has been that the emotions or feelings, like the opinions and abilities, require social evaluation when the emotion-producing situation is ambiguous or uninterpretable in terms of past experience. Much previous work has demonstrated that evaluation of the opinions and abilities is possible by means of social-comparison processes, and the schema developed from this work has led to the expectation that when discrepancies of emotional state exist, tendencies will arise to bring oneself into closer conformity with others, to change others, and to reject deviates as comparison points. Wrightsman's experiment on anxiety and the experiment on satiation conducted by Horwitz et al. have demonstrated the operation of such tendencies. Obviously these studies neatly support this view of emotion.

What about hunger? As with anxiety, there was a positive relationship between hunger and the affiliative tendency. But does it make sense to attempt to apply these notions of the evaluative process to a drive state such as hunger? We would suggest, though ever so gingerly, that it may. Though it has been traditional to treat emotional and drive states as distinct, it is no longer unusual to question the distinction. Woodworth (56), for one, has written, "Anyone will unhesitatingly classify as emotions: anger, fear, disgust, joy and sorrow; and as states of the organism: hunger, thirst, nausea, fatigue, drowsiness, intoxication. Now that physiology has revealed a peculiar organic state in fear and anger, why do we continue to call them emotions and deny that name to fatigue or drowsiness? It is hard to find a valid distinction." (P. 234.) But does it make sense to assume that there is any ambiguity or lack of understandability about as familiar a state as hunger? Perhaps, for hunger (even when it means merely doing without two meals) may not be at all a familiar experience to the contemporary American college student. If this set of notions is at all correct, it should be anticipated that those subjects who are familiar with hunger would have been less likely to choose a "Together" alternative. And the small bit of available evidence does tend to support this expectation. Before beginning the hunger-affiliation experiment, subjects filled in a brief questionnaire concerning their food habits. One question asked "How unusual is it for you to miss lunch?" and the subjects checked a six-point scale, ranging from "I very frequently miss lunch" to "I never miss lunch." We will consider those who indicate that they "very frequently," "quite often," or "occasionally" miss lunch as familiar with hunger feelings; and those who indicate that they "infrequently," "very rarely," or "never" miss lunch as unfamiliar with these feelings. In the high-hunger condition, 43 percent of subjects familiar ($N = 7$) with hunger chose "Together" and 79 percent of those unfamiliar ($N = 14$) with the state chose "Together." In the medium-hunger condition, 25 percent of the familiar group ($N = 4$) chose "Together" and 38 percent of unfamiliars ($N = 16$) did so. In low hunger, 29 percent of familiars ($N = 7$) and 31 percent of unfamiliars ($N = 13$) chose "Together." Clearly there is a stronger tendency for those unfamiliar with hunger to increase their affiliative choices as hunger increases than for those familiar with the sensation. The increase from low- to high-hunger conditions is 48 percent (significant at the .05 level by Exact test) for those unfamiliar with hunger feelings and only 14 percent (nonsignificant) for those familiar with such feelings. The fact that the proportions choosing "Together" are virtually identical in the low-hunger condition may be taken as evidence that there are no systematic differences between these two groups in their propensity

to choose "Together" when not hungry. Now, obviously any conclusion one is tempted to draw must be sharply tempered by the
clear possibility that those who at least occasionally do without
lunch simply feel less hungry. However, the fact that for such
subjects the rate of increase of affiliative choices is so very slow
after a full twenty hours of food deprivation (at which point, one
would guess, hunger feelings would be fairly intense for *all* subjects) might be considered tentative support for the contention that
it is the unfamiliarity of the experience of hunger that is the determining factor in the hunger-affiliation experiment. Clearly,
however, the point is still at issue and only further work which
partials out the effects of familiarity from those of experienced
intensity can clarify the relationship.

What about ordinal position? Can the various effects that have
been documented be subsumed under this slowly evolving schema?
It will be recalled that the diverse data on the effects of birth order
have all been interpreted in terms of a common notion—dependence or the degree to which the individual relies on others as
sources of approval, support, help, and reference. Now, clearly
people do differ in the extent to which they rely on others in evaluating themselves, their feelings, and their beliefs. Some people
seem sensitive to the lightest of social winds and appear unable to
make up their minds without strong social backing, while other
more solid types seem stubbornly independent. Designating this
dimension of reliance on others as dependence, it should be anticipated that first-born and only persons would place more reliance
on social means of evaluation than would later-born persons. Supporting evidence for this expectation comes from Ehrlich's and
Wrightsman's demonstrations that early-born subjects are more
socially influencible than later-born subjects. We are suggesting,
of course, that these results are the same order of phenomena as the
experimentally demonstrated relationship of ordinal position to
the affiliative reaction to anxiety. When placed in a situation some
aspect of which requires evaluation, early-born individuals are
more likely than later-born persons to seek out others as a means

of evaluation; when together with others in such a situation, early-born are more likely than later-born individuals to rely on others in evaluating their own opinions and emotional states.

Only one clear complication is evident in this formulation of the body of data presented in this volume. If the suggestion that the hunger-affiliation relationship is one more manifestation of evaluative needs is correct, it should be expected that the relationship of ordinal position to the affiliative tendency would be the same in the hunger experiments as in the anxiety experiments; that is, the greater the hunger, the greater the likelihood that first-born subjects will choose "Together." No such relationship is evident in the hunger experiment. Interpretation of this exception to our general scheme is, at this point, exceedingly difficult, for it could mean, among other things, that our speculations concerning the hunger-affiliation relationship are simply in error or that the effects of ordinal position are restricted to situations containing elements of anxiety. There is at present no compelling reason for preferring either one of these alternatives, and only further work can clarify the point.

Let us finally summarize the gist of these several studies and of our attempted formulation of these data. It has been our intention to examine circumstances which affect man's desires to be alone or with others. Substantively, it has been demonstrated primarily that affiliative tendencies increase with increasing anxiety and hunger, and that, for anxiety, ordinal position of birth is an effective discriminator of the magnitude of the affiliative tendency. The overall pattern of experimental results on the anxiety-affiliation relationship has narrowed down the interpretive alternatives to a point where it appears theoretically rewarding to formulate this body of findings as a manifestation of needs for anxiety reduction and of needs for self-evaluation; that is, ambiguous situations or feelings lead to a desire to be with others as a means of socially evaluating and determining the "appropriate" and proper reaction. This formulation is, to us, appealing, for if it proves correct it will not only delineate one class of circumstances which lead to the arousal of affiliative needs, but may, as well, permit the integration of the social determinants of opinion, ability, and emotion evaluation into a common conceptual scheme. Such a prospect is of course attractive, but let us be quite precise as to the extent to which such a formulation is supported by available evidence. There can be little doubt that the state of anxiety leads to the arousal of affiliative tendencies. The case for considering such findings as instances of the operation of evaluative needs rests largely on the experimental demonstration that anxiety is susceptible to social influence and that some degree of social interaction does result in increasing homogenization of feeling. Such results are encouraging, but clearly more evidence is needed. A definitive test of this explanation of the anxiety-affiliation relationship will require direct manipulation of the evaluative need. For the opinions and abilities numerous studies of social influence have demonstrated the fruitfulness of the assumption that evaluative needs do operate and that social-comparison processes provide one major channel for opinion and ability evaluation. There have, as yet, been no rigorous attempts to demonstrate that unclarity or uncertainty about an opinion or an ability leads to the arousal of affiliative tendencies. The gaps are evident.

References

1. Anson, P. F. *The quest of solitude*. New York: Dutton, 1932.
2. Atkinson, J. W. (ed.). *Motives in fantasy, action, and society*. Princeton: Van Nostrand, 1958.
3. Back, K. Influence through social communication. J. abnorm. soc. Psychol., 1951, *46*, 9–23.
4. Bakan, D. The relationship between alcoholism and birth rank. Quart. J. Stud. Alc., 1949, *10*, 434–40.
5. Baker, H. J., Decker, F. J., and Hill, A.S. A study of juvenile theft. J. educ. Res., 1929, *20*, 81–87.
6. Beller, E. K. Dependence and independence in young children. Doctoral dissertation, State University of Iowa, 1948.
7. Beller, E. K. Dependency and autonomous achievement striving related to orality and anality in early childhood. Child Developm., 1957, *28*, 287–315.
8. Burt, C. *The young delinquent*. New York: Appleton, 1925.
9. Cartwright, D., and Zander, A. (eds.). *Group dynamics: research and theory*. Evanston, Ill.: Row, Peterson, 1953.
10. Dean, Daphne A. The relation of ordinal position to personality in young children. Unpublished M.A. dissertation, State University of Iowa, 1947.
11. Draguet, R. *Les pères du désert*. Paris: Plon, 1949.
12. Dreyer, A. S. Aspiration behavior as influenced by expectation and group comparison. Hum. Relat., 1954, *7*, 175–90.
13. Ehrlich, Danuta. Determinants of verbal commonality and influencibility. Unpublished doctoral dissertation, University of Minnesota, 1958.
14. Faris, R. E. L. Cultural isolation and the schizophrenic personality. Amer. J. Sociol., 1934, *40*, 155–64.
15. Festinger, L. A theory of social comparison processes. Hum. Relat., 1954, *7*, 117–40.
16. Festinger, L., Gerard, H., et al. The influence process in the presence of extreme deviates. Hum. Relat., 1952, *5*, 327–46.

17. Festinger, L., Pepitone, A., and Newcomb, T. Some consequences of deindividuation in a group. J. abnorm. soc. Psychol., 1952, *47*, 382–89.

18. Festinger, L., Riecken, H., and Schachter, S. *When prophecy fails.* Minneapolis: University of Minnesota Press, 1956.

19. Festinger, L., Schachter, S., and Back, K. *Social pressures in informal groups.* New York: Harper, 1950.

20. Festinger, L., and Thibaut, J. Interpersonal communication in small groups. J. abnorm. soc. Psychol., 1951, *46*, 92–99.

21. Finneran, Mary P. Dependency and self-concept as functions of acceptance and rejection by others. Amer. Psychol., 1958, *13*, 332 (abstract).

22. French, Elizabeth G. Development of a measure of complex motivation. In J. W. Atkinson (ed.), *Motives in fantasy, action, and society.* Princeton: Van Nostrand, 1958, pp. 242–48.

23. French, Elizabeth G. Effects of the interaction of motivation and feedback on task performance. In J. W. Atkinson (ed.), *Motives in fantasy, action, and society.* Princeton: Van Nostrand, 1958.

24. Gewirtz, J. L. Dependent and aggressive interaction in young children. Doctoral dissertation, State University of Iowa, 1948.

25. Gibby, R. G., Stotsky, B. A., Hiler, E. W., and Miller, D. R. Validation of Rorschach criteria for predicting duration of therapy. J. consult. Psychol., 1954, *18*, 185–91.

26. Gilchrist, J. C. The formation of social groups under conditions of success and failure. J. abnorm. soc. Psychol., 1952, *47*, 174–87.

27. Haeberle, Ann. Interactions of sex, birth order and dependency with behavior problems and symptoms in emotionally disturbed preschool children. Paper read at East. Psychol. Assn., Philadelphia, Penn., 1958.

28. Hoffman, P. J., Festinger, L., and Lawrence, D. H. Tendencies toward group comparability in competitive bargaining. Hum. Relat., 1954, *7*, 141–59.

29. Hooker, Helen F. A study of the only child at school. J. genet. Psychol., 1931, *39*, 122–26.

30. Hoppe, F. Erfolg und misserfolg. Psychol. Forsch., 1930, *14*, 1–62.

31. Horwitz, M., Exline, R., Goldman, M., and Lee, F. Motivational effects of alternative decision-making processes in groups. Office of Naval Research Technical Report, June, 1953.

32. Levy, J. A quantitative study of behavior problems in relation to family constellation. Amer. J. Psychiat., 1931, *10*, 637–54.

33. Murphy, G., Murphy, Lois B., and Newcomb, T. M. *Experimental social psychology*. New York: Harper, 1937.

34. Rosenow, C., and Whyte, Anne H. The ordinal position of problem children. Amer. J. Orthopsychiat., 1931, *1*, 430–34.

35. Ruckmick, C. A. *The psychology of feeling and emotion*. New York: McGraw-Hill, 1936.

36. Schachter, S. Deviation, rejection and communication. J. abnorm. soc. Psychol., 1951, *46*, 190–207.

37. Schachter, S., and Burdick, H. A field experiment on rumor transmission and distortion. J. abnorm. soc. Psychol., 1955, *50*, 363–71.

38. Schachter, S., and Heinzelmann, F. Cognition, anxiety and time perception. In preparation.

39. Scheidlinger, S. *Psychoanalysis and group behavior: A study of Freudian group psychology*. New York: Norton, 1952.

40. Schönbach, P. Need, relevance of ideation, force and time estimation. Doctoral dissertation, University of Minnesota, 1956.

41. Sears, R. R. Ordinal position in the family as a psychological variable. Amer. sociol. Rev., 1950, *15*, 397–401.

42. Sears, R. R., Maccoby, E., and Levin, H. *Patterns of child rearing*. Evanston, Ill.: Row, Peterson, 1957.

43. Sears, R. R., Whiting, J. W. M., Nowles, V., and Sears, P. S. Some child-rearing antecedents of aggression and dependency in young children. Genet. Psychol. Monogr., 1953, *47*, 135–236.

44. Slawson, J. *The delinquent boy*. Boston: Gorham Press, 1926.

45. Sletto, R. F. Sibling position and juvenile delinquency. Amer. J. Sociol., 1934, *39*, 657–69.

46. Stagner, R., and Katzoff, E. T. Personality as related to birth order and family size. J. appl. Psychol., 1936, *20*, 340–46.

47. Taylor, J. A. A personality scale of manifest anxiety. J. abnorm. soc. Psychol., 1953, *48*, 285–90.

48. Thibaut, J. An experimental study of the cohesiveness of underprivileged groups. Hum. Relat., 1950, *3*, 251–78.

49. Thurstone, L. L., and Thurstone, Thelma G. A neurotic inventory. J. soc. Psychol., 1930, *1*, 3–30.

50. Torrance, E. P. A psychological study of American jet aces. Paper read at West. Psychol. Assn., Long Beach, California, 1954.

51. Torrance, E. P. Survival stresses and food problems. Paper read at the Symposium on Stress as Applied to Food Problems. Quartermaster Research and Development Command, Natick, Mass., 1957.

52. Weissberg, A. *The accused*. New York: Simon and Schuster, 1951.

53. Whiting, J. W. M., and Child, I. L. *Child training and personality*. New Haven: Yale University Press, 1953.

54. Wiener, D. N., and Stieper, D. R. Psychometric prediction of length and outcome of outpatient therapy. Monograph in preparation.

55. Witty, P. A. "Only" and "intermediate" children of high school ages. Psychol. Bull., 1934, *31*, 734.

56. Woodworth, R. S. *Experimental Psychology*. New York: Holt, 1938.

57. Woodworth, R. S., and Marquis, D. G. *Psychology*. New York: Holt, 1948.

58. Woodworth, R. S., and Schlosberg, H. *Experimental Psychology*. New York: Holt, 1954.

59. Wrightsman, L. The effects of small-group membership on level of concern. Unpublished doctoral dissertation. University of Minnesota, 1959.

60. Young, P. T. *Emotion in man and animal*. New York: Wiley, 1943.

Index

DATE DUE